FINDING LOVE LATER IN LIFE

Brunch at the Crooked Oak Café

Ron Crawford

© 2023
Published in the United States by Nurturing Faith, Macon, GA.
Nurturing Faith is a book imprint of Good Faith Media (goodfaithmedia.org).
Library of Congress Cataloging-in-Publication Data is available.

ISBN: 978-1-63528-217-7

All rights reserved. Printed in the United States of America.

Cover image by Jaqueline Pelzer on Unsplash.

About the Author

Ron Crawford lives on three and a half acres of paradise in Powhatan County, Virginia, with his wife Melanie. Ron stays busy with keeping up the property, woodworking, family, travel, and writing. His latest adventure is scuba diving. In his previous life before retirement, Ron was a pastor and seminary president. In Powhatan, he is mostly known as Melanie's husband; she is deeply involved in the Powhatan Free Clinic and is a vocal advocate for those who could use a little help.

Contents

Introduction 1

Finding the Café 3

Mia 11

Carlos 29

Carlos and Mia 47

Sara 55

Walt 75

Sara and Walt 95

Brunch Conclusion 105

Introduction

It is possible to find vibrant love in the seventh decade of life. Two couples shared brunch and the joy of a surprise wedding at the Crooked Oak Restaurant. This book describes the encounter and the back stories that made the event so memorable and hopeful. This is an honest book affirming that many people find themselves unpaired in their sixties either through divorce or the death of a spouse. Yet it also affirms the adage, "Once in a while, in the middle of an ordinary life, love gives us a fairy tale."

Disappointment, hardship, and even tragedy set the stage for every fairy tale. The four characters in this book share a legacy of struggle though they come from different backgrounds: Puerto Rican American, Armenian American and Anglo-American. They were all also surprised by finding enduring love in a later chapter of life.

These four characters are real people with distinct family and national heritages, and the historical details are true. As with all good stories, however, some of the events in this book are embellishments. Some happenings are contemporaneous with the characters and "artistically" interwoven into their lives in the style of *Forrest Gump*. Some stories were imported from the life experience of other people and placed in the saga of our four characters. And, of course, the names of the four characters have been changed, else they would be swarmed by adoring fans when this book becomes a best seller.

Ultimately, this is a hopeful book. Finding yourself unpaired in a later chapter of life can be desperately unsettling. When you have had a partner for most, if not all, of your adult life, finding yourself alone is disconcerting and disorientating. Many people choose to remain unattached in later life, as being with someone is exceedingly complex. When you are young, you fall in love and grow up together. When you are old, you have adult children with opinions, a tax advisor, property, financial accounts, and long memories of being with another person.

There are plenty of good reasons to remain unpaired in later life. Even so, sometimes "love gives us a fairy tale."

Finding the Café

"So where the heck is the Crooked Oak Café?" I posed this rhetorical question out loud to myself, or maybe to the universe. I was seeking clarity more than an audible answer.

When I first arranged the meeting at the café, I thought it was in the little town of Hillsville, Virginia, but I had apparently overlooked the café's geographical location. Selecting the location for our meeting proved to be more challenging than I had thought.

For Sara and I, brunch at the café extended a relaxing few days away from the hustle and bustle of ordinary life. In late August, we had planned our getaway to the four-and-a-half-star Homestead Resort in Hot Springs, Virginia. A few days of hiking and being pampered by the resort staff proved delightful and refreshing. When we planned the trip, we had anticipated staying in Hot Springs as long as we could and then planned to return to our home in Powhatan, Virginia, to resume progress on our list of house projects to complete before the arrival of colder weather. In retiring, Sara and I had traded professional lives for the more physical labor of refurbishing our new home and property (3.5 acres, mostly hardwood trees).

Shortly after planning the Hot Springs trip and contemplating how to finish our projects, I contacted Mia about her planned wedding for December 12. I had gladly agreed to officiate at Mia and Carlos's wedding when I last saw them in Orlando in January; thus, the December 12 marriage ceremony had been on my calendar for eight months. But those wedding plans had been set before the arrival of the brutal COVID-19 virus, which had demolished everything normal about day-to-day life in America. So I sent Mia a text to confirm plans for the December wedding. I shared my sense of excitement about her upcoming marriage and said I would do whatever was needed to make the day a success; in effect, I suggested that I would happily drive the twelve hours to Orlando, Florida, for the wedding. I naturally assumed the ceremony would be scaled back, impacted by COVID-19 restrictions like everything else.

Mia responded via text that she and Carlos were still considering options regarding the wedding. She texted me again several days later, noting that she and Carlos were planning a week's vacation near Fancy Gap, Virginia, and wondered if Sara and I might be able to see them during that timeframe. I was surprised by the timing of their trip; Sara and I would be in Hot Springs ending our getaway at the same time. I texted back that Sara and I could meet them either Friday afternoon or evening, or for brunch on Saturday.

Secretly, I hoped Mia would embrace the Friday option, as that would mean Sara and I could simply swing by Fancy Gap on the way home, thus only extending our trip by a handful of hours. But Mia opted for Saturday brunch. I texted that I would find a place to meet and get back to her with the details.

"Babe," I called out to Sara. "They opted for Saturday brunch."

"Oh, well," she replied. "That means another night away from *Green Acres*. It will be worth it to see them."

I couldn't help chuckling to myself. Sara and I were still learning about one another. We were only two and a half years into our marriage and still discovering things about each other.

Sara was proving to be much more of a homebody than I would have ever imagined. I was sixty-five when we started dating. She is five years younger; I will let you do the math, as I have learned better than to announce the age of my wife. In our dating life, and in her professional life as a Speech Language Pathologist, she was always on the go, with "places to go and people to see." To my amazement, that changed when we bought our first home together in Powhatan, Virginia. Our home is part of one small development of forty-eight homes, placed on three and a half acres between our development and the neighboring one of sixty homes. We may be among one hundred homes, but it sure feels isolated when we turn off the paved road onto our gravel lane, 250 yards long.

While still working as a therapist, Sara had a busy, bustling schedule. She worked in home health, meaning she provided therapy in private homes. She saw patients on a strict schedule: fifty minutes of therapy, then out the door and a mad dash to the next house and patient.

Every Sunday evening, she made phone calls and scheduled patients for the week, accounting for the driving distance between their individual homes. Sara prided herself in being an advocate for her patients. Sometimes this meant she was on the phone to a doctor's office as she drove to the next patient's home, requesting additional medications or services to be provided to the patient she had just seen. She was also known for encouraging (her word) or fussing at (my word) adult children for not taking better care of their parents. In her professional line of work, Sara was a force to be reckoned with. Yet she described turning onto our gravel driveway as entering a piece of heaven.

Six months into our shared life in the new home, Sara announced that we were going to call our little piece of heaven Green Acres. I smiled, thinking about all the ways the reference to the TV show Green Acres seemed fitting: the place we bought was in need of repair and an extra portion of loving care; I was a pastor for most of my career and ended my professional life as a seminary president; and Sara, while a no-nonsense medical person, also had a glitzy, flamboyant Eva Gabor within her that emerged from time to time, especially when we attended the opera. The only obvious difference in our Green Acres storyline was that I didn't seem to have Oliver's influence over Lisa when it came to my wife. In the TV series, Oliver (Eddie Albert) would make decisions for himself *and* his wife (Eva Gabor), like the decision to move from a high-rise apartment in Manhattan to a broken-down shack in Hooterville. My relationship with Sara was different. She and I once rented a Jet Ski when vacationing in Florida. The guy at the rental place looked at me and asked, "What do you want in a Jet Ski, stability or speed?" Sara responded, "Speed." She drove the Jet Ski. I sat behind her holding on for dear life—which is what I have been doing since I met her!

In selecting a place for brunch with Carlos and Mia, I wanted a restaurant that would provide some measure of privacy. A Google search yielded an interesting list of possibilities: Shoney's, Lake View Motel, Earl's Diner, County Line Café, Crooked Oak Café, Cavalier Café, and Aunt Bea's BBQ. Some of the restaurants didn't open until 11 A.M., which made me wonder why they came up on a breakfast search. Several of the restaurants were not listed on Yelp. As Mia and I had agreed on a 10:30 brunch, part of my challenge was finding a restaurant that served breakfast until at least 11:00 A.M.

Crooked Oak Café met that criterion and had good reviews. I texted Mia with the name of the restaurant and its Hillsville address. In my haste, I made assumptions about its actual location. Instead of being in Hillsville, Google Maps identified it as being located 8.5 miles outside Hillsville on US 58 East. Thankfully, Sara was ready to go, and we had time to drive the distance and still arrive for our 10:30 brunch.

"What's with the name Crooked Oak?" I asked Sara, or maybe the universe, still a bit peeved that I had selected a location outside of town.

"You're asking me?" she replied. "Didn't you select the café?"

I grumbled and then mused a bit about the cafe's name as I drove. The name Crooked Oak seemed odd. Florida has its water oak or live oak trees, honed and adapted to passing hurricanes. The oaks of Florida tend to have thick and long branches, with small branches growing off the stout primary ones. In hurricane-force winds, the small branches easily break off, leaving the sturdy, thick branches with greatly reduced wind resistance—thus ensuring that the larger branches are not twisted off the trunk. In Virginia, oaks are known as tall trees with straight trunks. I wondered why the café owners took on the name Crooked Oak.

As I learned later, Crooked Oak is the name of the very rural community surrounding the restaurant. There is a Crooked Oak Methodist Church, a Crooked Oak Missionary Baptist Church, a Crooked Oak Road, and a Crooked Oak Auto Repair Shop that looked abandoned.

Historically, the Crooked Oak Community built up along the ten-mile twists and turns of Pine Creek, which flows from its headwaters in the midst of a huge stand of pine trees until it pours into Big Reed Island Creek. The Crooked Oak Community was named for its abundance of black oak trees. Black oaks are recognizable for their irregular, even unruly branches. White oaks and red oaks, both abundant in central Virginia, are tall and straight; their branches veer off from the main trunk but grow relatively straight up toward the heavens.

Black oak branches grow more like hickory tree branches, twisting and turning at right angles as they grow for no apparent reason, hence black oaks are known for their crooked branches. White and red oaks grow well in forest settings with rich soil where numerous competing trees grow upward toward a canopy. Black oaks have adapted to poor soil conditions, and so they tend to grow alone or at some distance from other trees, as the quality of the soil simply cannot sustain a plentiful number of trees. Early eighteenth century settlers in the Crooked Oak area either embraced the poor soil and harsh winters or else moved on to kinder environments like the lush New River Valley farther west.

As I learned later, Crooked Oak had an interesting footnote in the international headlines of 1912. The story of the Hillsville Massacre rivaled that of the sinking of the *Titanic* that same year and became the stuff of legend for several decades. Floyd Allen was charged with "illegal rescue of prisoners," as the Virginia statute put it at the time. In a jury trial, Allen was pronounced guilty as charged. The judge in the case then denied two motions from the defense that the verdict be set aside and also a request for bail. The judge ordered Allen to be held in the local jail as he awaited transfer to a state penitentiary. Legend has it that Allen stood and said, "Gentlemen, I just ain't a goin'." That is when the shooting began! For the next sixty seconds, the courtroom became a shooting gallery. The judge, the sheriff, the Commonwealth's Attorney, and a juror were killed. Two dozen others were injured.

Virginia law in 1912 noted that when a sheriff died, all his deputies lost their legal powers; thus, there was no legal entity in Hillsville to arrest people for the massacre in the courtroom. The state's governor intervened and authorized the Baldwin-Felts Detective Agency in Roanoke to hunt down those still at large. Several fugitives were apprehended quickly. Wesley Edwards and Sidna Allen were far more difficult to track down given their familiarity with the area and the hospitality provided by relatives and sympathetic friends. To make a long story short, the two were finally apprehended in a smokehouse in the Crooked Oak community. Apparently, the independent-minded folks of Crooked Oak had sheltered the fugitives for weeks.

Our twelve-minute drive to the Crooked Oak Café revealed a beautiful if isolated stretch of road. There were few dwellings sighted and fewer intersecting roads.

The café was located out in the middle of what seemed to be nowhere; it was the only building in sight. It stood close to the road, giving evidence that it had been in place for a long time before the widening of US 58. A few cars were parked in the sparsely graveled lot, and a few motorcycles were parked near the entrance. The building could have greatly benefitted from a fresh coat of paint. It looked like a small one-story warehouse, like multi-windowed textile plant buildings long idle as the industry left for overseas operations.

I was beginning to think my selection of the café was a mistake. It did not look like a place for a cozy brunch with friends.

I held the door for Sara. As she walked in, I quickly surveyed the place; it was a large space with outdated booths, chairs, and tables. It felt like one of those modern urban retro diners, except I knew it wasn't. The inside of this café had been the same for forty years or more.

There was one lone customer, an older gentleman chatting with a waitress long after he had finished his breakfast. Several restaurant staff members took notice of us as we entered the café; it seemed as if they were expecting us. Carlos and Mia were already seated in a booth. A waitress smiled at us as we walked by as if she knew a secret we were about to discover.

Sara and I greeted our friends and then took our seats across from them. We began peppering them with questions. What brings you to Fancy Gap? Where are you staying? How long did it take you to drive from Orlando? How are the kids doing? Of course, they had questions for us as well: Where did you stay last night? How far is Richmond from here? When are you headed home? How are your children doing? Why do they call it Fancy Gap?

The four of us talked a mile a minute and spoke over one another like good friends do who have not seen each other in months. Sara and I talked about our adventure that morning finding the café, after first assuming it was in the town of Hillsville. Carlos and Mia outdid us as they described "coming over the mountain" from Fancy Gap, twisting and turning on narrow roads, even making a wrong turn up a driveway with a sign that read, "We shoot trespassers."

While we had menus, we paid no attention to them. The waitress came by for drink orders, and after a little discussion we placed our food orders as well. In the brief moment of quiet, Sara could contain herself no longer. "So tell us about the wedding plans!"

Mia responded by extending her left hand across the table revealing a beautiful engagement ring and…a wedding band?

Mia

It was 1511 and the destination was Los Rabanos, Boriken, the Land of the Valiant Cacique. Aixa was twice over a cacique, the title used by the Taino People to designate the regional chief or the wife of the regional chief. She advised her husband, Gueybana, against leading his tribe into open conflict with the Spanish. Her words fell on deaf ears.

The battle of Yaguecas went poorly for her tribesmen, as many were killed, including her husband. Now, the widowed Aixa was a cacique in her own right, leading what remained of her tribe deep into the central mountains of Boriken. As a Taino with a long royal maternal bloodline, she refused to acknowledge the new name Spanish explorers hung on her beloved Boriken like a cheap necklace—Puerto Rico.

The Taino rebellion of 1511, encompassing eight years thereafter, was the last meaningful organized resistance to the Spanish conquest of modern-day Puerto Rico. After the defeat at Yaguecas, the island-wide coalition of Tainos evaporated into small regional battles. The Taino rebellion led to several outcomes for the once proud natives: many died in battle; many more were taken into slavery by Spanish victors; too many died by tribal-wide suicide instead of embracing slavery and the loss of their proud heritage; and others migrated to other islands or into the deep interior of the island.

While Taino tribes were given a handful of terrible functional options by the Spanish, Cacique Aixa intuitively knew that migrating (not retreating) into the deep central highlands of Boriken provided the only "hopeful" future for her people.

Eighteen miles separated the broad plains of Guaynia (modern Guayanilla) from the mountain outpost of Los Rabanos; but it might as well have been 180 miles given the extreme terrain. Los Rabanos was a small mining outpost along the Rio Guayo River. At Los Rabanos, the river was barely 10 feet wide; it flowed northward and then westward as a tributary of the Rio Grande de Anasco. This mountainous terrain made Los Rabanos one of the most isolated regions on the entire island.

Cacique Aixa saw possibilities in the isolation; her people could live in peace and continue to celebrate their rich heritage.

Life in Los Rabanos required Aixa's tribe to learn anew subsistence living in harsh conditions; such was the price of freedom in her time. Eventually, Los Rabanos became a robust mountain village. Within a decade of relocating, residents began trading agricultural goods in the markets of surrounding towns and cities: Utuado, Lares, Adjuntas, Penuelas, Yauco, Ponce, and, to a lesser degree, Guayanilla. Oranges and bananas grew reasonably well in the Los Rabanos area; coffee grew extremely well.

The descendants of Aixa's modest tribe continued to adapt to the changing environment of the island. In its isolated perch, Los Rabanos escaped much of the social upheaval that gripped the island over the coming centuries: Spanish overlords reforming and re-reforming the island's political landscape from generation to generation; sugar plantations arising in coastal areas, built on the backs of slaves; and the Lares Uprising of 1866 and its political aftermath.

The uprising in Lares did have an indirect influence on Los Rabanos. After the uprising was defeated by Spanish authorities, a Lares resident, Juan Castaner, moved to the Los Rabanos area and bought a small plot of land to begin growing coffee. At the time, in 1868, virtually no one in Los Rabanos took note of the newcomer. Over the coming decades, Castaner build one of the largest agricultural enterprises in all of Puerto Rico; by the onset of the Great Depression in 1927, he had more than 1,500 acres committed to coffee production.

The Great Depression drastically reduced the worldwide demand for coffee. Even so, coffee production in Los Rabanos continued on a much smaller scale. This meant that Castaner laid off many of his seasonal harvesters and focused employees on harvesting the crop and removing the ripened coffee cherries (beans in hull) from under the trees, else the soil would become toxic for growing the following year's crop. The Castaner hacienda became a gathering place for the desperate in the Los Rabanos community: Juan Castaner made sure every former employee had food and the basic necessities of life. In spite of all he did to ensure the future of his coffee empire, the Great Depression virtually destroyed everything Juan Castaner had built over a lifetime.

The decade of the 1930s brought significant change to Los Rabanos. The Puerto Rican Reconstruction Administration (funded by the federal government's New Deal) created Lago (lake) Guayo just downstream from Los Rabanos and provided major financial investments in the town. The descendants of Juan Castaner parceled out the farm to previous workers and local residents; they also sold the Castaner hacienda to the Puerto Rican government. And, perhaps most significant, the village leaders renamed Los Rabanos as Castaner.

Castaner struggled to gain its footing after the Great Depression. The efficiencies of a large farm enterprise were completely lost as self-employed farmers grew overwhelmed with too many coffee trees to care for, too few ways to get their product to markets, and virtually no capital to save their modest farming operations when demand for coffee wavered.

Decades stretched into other decades as the plight of Castaner residents never seemed to recover. These were hard and difficult times for the mountain region that had been such a welcome sight for Aixa's tribe centuries before.

Mia was born in 1958 into this cauldron of perpetual poverty. Mia's mother's heritage traced back to the Taino clan and Cacique Aixa. For centuries, Mia's mother's people had made a home for themselves in Los Rabanos, meager as it was in the 1950s. Mia's father, Angel, traced his heritage through the extended clan of Juan Castaner to Lares, and before that Mayaguez—on the western coast of Puerto Rico. Mayaguez was a once-sleepy village transformed by sugar trade in the early nineteenth century.

Mayaguez was founded on September 18, 1760, by two pairs of brothers who migrated from the Canary Islands. Twenty-nine days earlier, on August 21, 1760, a lot in the center of what would become the city was consecrated Nuestra Senora de la Candelaria (Our Lady of Candelaria), named for the Feast of Candelaria commemorating Christ's presentation at the temple. A modest Catholic cathedral was completed on the site in 1780. Mia's father's family claimed that a distant ancestor placed the keystone in the arch over the altar in the original church building. They were deeply committed Catholics.

In many ways, the complexity of Puerto Rico's past was embodied in Mia. She was a descendant of both the noble native population and of Spanish adventurers whose religious fervor sought to create a better world.

Of course, the infant Mia knew nothing of these colliding worlds. Rather, she grew up in a small mountain village with an angry, jilted mother and an absent father. Early on, it became obvious that Mia's parents were not headed for marital bliss. Their differences, rooted in deep family heritages, soon pulled the marriage apart. Ever the adventurer, Mia's father first moved to San Juan and later to Brooklyn, New York.

Mia had no memory of her father before the divorce and before his departure from Castaner. She met him for the first time when she was eight years old. Her father returned to visit his parents in Castaner. An aunt took Mia to meet her father at her grandparents' home. For Mia, her father was more a curiosity than anything else. She remembered little from their first meeting, except that he seemed tall and walked with a confident grace. Mia was surprised to sense that her father was a gentle spirit. Mia's mother had always described him as a worthless, no-count, lazy, irresponsible liar. Sometimes in a sense of despair Mia's jilted mother would rant about how Angel thought too highly of himself—how he claimed he was a success, but no residue of that success ever made its way back to support his daughter.

For her own part, Mia always thought of her father as a mystery. It was hard not to embrace her mother's interpretation of her father, yet Mia had trouble reconciling that harsh reality with the gentle soul she sensed in her father when she met him. This internal mystery about her father only increased when she saw him for a second time when she was twelve. On that occasion, he seemed affectionate and proud of his daughter *and* enamored with his life in New York.

Early on, it became apparent that little Mia was going places. She had a drive and determination rarely seen in children in Castaner. She was always the first in line, often the first in her class, and too often the first one in trouble for pushing parameters. In the small town of Castaner she was known as the organizer of games. Her favorite children's games were "Uno, Dos, Tres, Calabaza" and "La Gallinita Ciega."

Uno, Dos, Tres, Calabaza was much like the US game "Red Light, Green Light." One of the children would stand with her back to the other children, who stood far away. The one child would count out "Uno, dos, tres," and the other children would run toward the first child in hopes of touching her before she turned around. If the first child called out "calabaza" (freeze) and caught anyone moving, she would say their names and they would have to go back to the starting line. The object was to eventually get close enough to touch the person who was "it." Then, the game would start over with a new child calling out, "Uno, dos, tres."

Mia was especially good at sensing when to stop and stand still a split second before the other child called out "calabaza" and quickly turned to catch other children moving.

Her other favorite game, La Gallinita Ciega translates as "The Blind Little Hen." In the game, children stand in a big circle. One child begins the game by being the hen, who is blindfolded, turned in a circle three times, and then led by someone else into the middle of the circle. The hen must find another person outlining the circle and, by touching the arms and face, guess who the person is. If the guess is correct, then the two change places and the game begins again. If incorrect, the hen is allowed to move around the circle until she guesses someone correctly. Part of the fun of the game is to remain quiet and disguise yourself by standing taller or shorter and disfiguring your face.

As an older child and teenager, Mia especially loved music. Her first love was *Jibaros* music. *Jibaros*, the Taino word for "People of the Forest," came to refer to the musical style that was rooted in the mountain regions of Puerto Rico. Originally, *Jibaros* was a derogatory term used to refer to the poor and ignorant people who lived in the mountains. During the Spanish occupation, the government prohibited *Jibaros* from attending school and limited their daily activity.

Thus, Jibaros music tended to focus on themes of liberation. In addition, the music tended to be rowdy.

As she grew older, Mia was introduced to Bomba, a mixture of Spanish, African, and Native Taino Music. Bomba is a musical style borrowed from seventeenth century West Africans who were brought to the island as slaves. In Bomba dance, and other Caribbean dance styles, the woman's lifting of her skirt to show her legs and/or slip was said to mock European ladies and plantation landowners for their way of dress. Bomba tended to be sassy. For Mia, dance was rooted in the complexity of her heritage and was always a way to act out her inner feelings and energy.

The Puerto Rican world Mia grew up in was a mixture of rich cultural traditions (Tiano, Spanish, and African). This was especially true of religion in Castaner. Historically, the town owed its roots to Taino religious traditions. Taino religion is complex and well developed, with an account of human origins and a cosmology including a long list of supernatural deities. Individual deities rule some aspect of daily life and the world of nature.

While the highest deity is supposed to be the invisible *Yocaju Bagua Maorocoti*, the supreme maker, in fact the mother of *Yocaju*, was worshipped more widely. She was referred to as *Atabey*, or *Yermar Guacar Apito*, or *Zuimaco*. In all likelihood, Taino religion originally was a matrilineal tradition (with a goddess as the supreme being), and *Yocaju* (a male figure) was elevated in importance as the Spanish presence in the area began to influence the way natives thought of their religion.

In addition to *Yocaju* and *Atabey*, Tainos worship many lesser gods as well as the spirits of dead ancestors. They believe that the dead, invisible, walk around among the living. Thus, the spirit world is interwoven with, and part of, the present moment. The Catholic (Spanish) tradition's esteem for and veneration of Saints may have facilitated an acceptance of Catholicism among the Taino native population.

Mia loved to tell a story about her grandmother that illustrates the spiritualistic background she inherited. Her mother's mother was as much a Taino as any who ever lived. She was short, had wonderful copper-colored skin and straight black hair, and displayed the broad face with prominent cheekbones that was long associated with the Taino tradition. On one occasion she attended a traditional Taino tribal celebration. These were gatherings designed to reinforce Taino myths, traditions, and history. They always include tribal *areytos*, or dances, and *cohiba*, whereby the shaman inhaled smoke from a mixture of herbs, spices, dried mushrooms, and tobacco to induce a trance.

Apparently, Grandma got into the *cohiba* herself and entered a trance. She proceeded to take off her clothes. In her defense, the native Tainos did not wear clothing at all except for the *nagua* (half-slip) worn by married women. Grandma's dance continued long after other celebrants headed home. Very late into the evening, Grandma ended up at the door of the home of the Baptist preacher in Castaner. The pastor and his wife took Grandma in and draped a blanket around her. When she was finally released from the trance, she was deeply emotional, crying and completely humiliated by her behavior. The pastor interpreted her behavior as a spiritual crisis and offered her a better way—Jesus Christ. The end result of the evening was that Grandma became a Baptist, embraced Baptist theology, and faithfully attended the local Baptist church for the rest of her life.

Mia's mother was not happy to learn that her daughter was entertaining ideas of moving to San Juan to seek a college education; the news seemed to stir painful memories of being abandoned that had not softened over the years. Mia's mother made leaving home for San Juan difficult. Even so, Mia struck out for her new future, following her own dreams for a better life. She enrolled in the Universidad de Puerto Rico Rio Piedras Campus.

While Mia had graduated at the top of her class in Castaner, she was not quite ready for the academic rigor of the oldest, largest, and most prestigious educational institution in the Caribbean. She began catching up in her second semester, however, and soon resumed her natural place as one of the best students in her class. For Mia, and for most students at her university, college was work and more work. She studied hard and then worked a part-time job to pay for her college education. During one semester she worked two part-time jobs to make ends meet. During the summers, she took a light load in summer school, worked a full-time job, and worked her part-time job on weekends.

In her final year at the university, Mia met and fell in love with a dashing young military man. Jorge was a native of San Juan and was home on temporary leave from his military service. Mia's graduation from Universidad de Puerto Rico coincided with Jorge's completion of his military service. The couple married and settled in San Juan; Mia worked at San Juan Municipal Hospital and Jorge pursued his interest in becoming a pastor.

Jorge did not grow up in a particularly religious family, but he was impressed with a chaplain during his tour of military duty. Jorge seemed to be a bit of a natural in pastoral work, though it was obvious to the careful eye that he was seeking solace in religion.

Jorge enrolled in the military as the war in Vietnam was unwinding; he arrived in Vietnam in early 1974 and was assigned service alongside South Vietnam forces. It was a devastating year for South Vietnam forces as they were repeatedly overrun by the People's Army of Vietnam (North Vietnam forces), which eventually took the city of Saigon on April 30, 1975. In the chaos of that year, Jorge experienced firsthand the trauma and devastation of war. It left an indelible impression on him and often resulted in sleepless nights.

In the military, Jorge was assigned to the crew of a Boeing Sea Knight Cargo Helicopter; it was the CH-46D model. His particular helicopter had been upgraded from a 46A model with the inclusion of modified rotors and more powerful engines. Jorge was delighted with this assignment as it meant he served on a helicopter focused on moving supplies from ships to American bases in Vietnam, usually miles away from the front lines of battle.

While his assignment was rather routine, his fellow crew members were anything but routine; Ny, Tex, Moose, and Juan made for a cohesive crew who knew how to land, load, and lift the freight. Ny was the captain and pilot, Ny being a short version of his surname, Nystul. Tex was the co-pilot, so named for his hometown of El Paso. Moose was named for his realistic imitation of a moose's call; he was from the tiny village of Malta, Montana—population 2,195. Jorge picked up the nickname Juan as he was originally from San Juan.

Most of Jorge's service was uneventful: landing, loading, lifting, flying, landing, and unloading. All of that changed in the eleventh hour of the withdrawal of personnel from Saigon in April 1975. Without notice, Jorge's helicopter was pressed into service on the afternoon of April 29 as the North Vietnamese army rapidly closed in on Saigon. Most US troops had already left the country, as the US had been winding down its military force for many months. The US left in place a dozen crews to assist with cargo transportation matters: landing, loading, lifting.

In the frantic chaos of April 28 and 29, all available US helicopters in the region had been reassigned to assist with the evacuation of American and South Vietnamese citizens from Saigon. This involved landing at one of the bases in Saigon and then transporting people to the evacuation fleet off South Vietnam. In all, over 7,000 people were evacuated in a little more than twenty-four hours.

Navigating landings on the base was the easy part. The military bases were large, so there were no less than ten sites, some makeshift, where helicopters would land. People would then run in groups of thirty to thirty-five to get on the helicopters. As soon as they boarded, the helicopter would rev its powerful engines and begin to lift off, headed as quickly as possible to the evacuation fleet. Jorge's crew made four relatively flawless trips. The tricky part was navigating the landing on the ship. Jorge's helicopter was assigned to the USS *Hancock*, an aircraft carrier. The fighter jets that would normally occupy the deck and hull of the massive carrier had all been sent to a base in Can Tho, the southernmost part of Vietnam, so they were still close enough if needed in the declining situation in Saigon. Instead of fighter jets, the carrier's huge deck was covered in all manner of helicopters. Many of the helicopters were of the South Vietnamese variety, commandeered and flown by people desperately escaping the collapse of Saigon.

As Jorge's helicopter was landing on the USS *Hancock*'s deck for the fourth time, the ship's crew had already begun pushing helicopters off the deck and overboard into the sea to make room for other helicopters to land. Some of the abandoned helicopters sank almost immediately. Others were kept afloat for thirty minutes or more by pockets of air, sometimes just below the surface of the water.

When Jorge's helicopter returned with its fifth load, the deck of the carrier was so full of helicopters there literally was no space to land. Even though the helicopter was almost out of fuel, Ny decided to hover just off the deck to wait for another helicopter to leave before landing and unloading. Jorge instinctively ran to the back of the helicopter to visually check on the level of fuel in the tank; the dial on the pilot's control panel had been pegged to "E" for some time. Jorge discovered the tank was empty and the helicopter was literally flying on the fuel in the lines going to each engine. He called out for Ny to swing the helicopter around so that the loading dock at the rear of the helicopter was facing the edge of the carrier deck. His idea was to lower the helicopter so that passengers could literally jump from the helicopter to the carrier deck. With little choice, Ny did just as Jorge suggested, and all thirty-six of the passengers made it to safety. Having unloaded, Ny maneuvered his helicopter farther away from the carrier, waiting for his turn to land.

The Ch-46 model helicopter has one fuel tank and two engines, one at each end of the helicopter. Engines rarely run out of fuel at the same moment. In the case of Jorge's helicopter, the front engine stopped a few seconds before the back engine, and so the helicopter plunged toward the sea front first and struck one of the helicopters in the water that had been pushed over earlier. The collision created an explosion, as there was still fuel in the tank of the abandoned helicopter.

Jorge remembered the collision and hitting his head as he was literally thrown against the wall separating the pilot's cabin from the loading section. With the collision, a huge fireball engulfed the pilot's cabin and reached back into the loading section. The blast immediately killed the pilot and co-pilot. Jorge received significant but not fatal burns to his chest and left hand. As Jorge was regaining consciousness and struggling to keep his head above the turbulent water, he noticed the helicopter was rapidly sinking into the ocean nose first, leaving the rear loading dock open to the sky. He held his breath and waited.

As the helicopter was sinking around him, he caught sight of someone, or something, to his left. He instinctively grabbed hold of a mass of camouflage clothing, which happened to contain unconscious Moose. That Jorge and Moose floated while the helicopter sank all around them is nothing short of a miracle. Within thirty minutes, both were rescued from the water. Unfortunately, two crew members were lost. Capt. William Nystul and Lt. Michael Shea were the last two US casualties of the Vietnam War.

The experience of the crash became seared into Jorge's mind. Over and over again in his sleep or in flashbacks he relived the crash: being slammed into the wall of the pilot's cabin, hitting his head and losing consciousness, and then seeing flames all around him. While his chest was burned worse than his left hand and index finger, his slightly disfigured index finger seemed to be the constant reminder of the tragedy. It was always present and easily seen, even when he was holding and preaching from a Bible.

It is a great sadness that Jorge failed to appreciate what he did right that day. It was his idea to hover near the carrier so thirty-six people could jump to safety. It was his instinct to grab a passing mass of clothing and potentially saved a crewmate. Even so, all he could see and focus on was the collision and the ball of fire that took two friends. In subsequent years, Jorge's therapists encouraged him to seek his medical records, thinking they might reveal brain damage from the collision. Jorge never did. From the trauma of that day, and maybe a brain injury, Jorge never fully recovered. Rather, from that day forward his own life seemed to careen farther and farther afield. Ever so slowly, he seemed to lose a small piece of himself with every dream and flashback.

The happiest years of his marriage to Mia were the years they lived in San Juan.

Jorge found employment at Primera Iglesia Bautista de Rio Piedras (First Baptist Church of Rio Piedras) as a mission minister assistant. The church dated its beginnings to the mission work of the American Baptist Home Mission Society (American Baptist denomination) in 1899. The congregation was the mother church of most of the other Baptist churches in Puerto Rico, and its vibrant congregation continued to thrive into the late 1970s. At the time, Rev. Cristino Diaz Montanez was the pastor and the church had just settled into a new sanctuary (1977) on Calle Brumbaugh, just south of Universidad de Puerto Rico—Recinto de Rio Piedras. The church was a lively center of Latino life in the larger San Juan area. Jorge's work was primarily with smaller mission congregations sponsored by the mother church in the city's areas of poverty. Jorge enjoyed the personal connections he made with poor people in depressed areas of San Juan and the lively worship of a large and thriving city church.

Mia's work as a nurse at San Juan Municipal Hospital provided meaningful work and an amazing health care environment as the Municipal Hospital was in a cluster, or consortium, of hospitals including The School of Pharmacy—University of Puerto Rico, University District Hospital, and Industrial Hospital. While the work itself tended to be routine, partly because of her modest experience, the larger environment was nothing less than cutting-edge and exciting.

The happy couple lived in a small rented apartment on Luisa Street down in the heart of Condado. Given the bus service, they both enjoyed easy commutes to work. The Condado setting was a thriving historic area with loads of commercial activity and several nearby parks. On days off, the pair enjoyed long walks in Jaime Benitez Park, Ventana al Mar, or, a little farther, Playita del Condado. When they sought something different, they would take the short bus ride down Avenida Ashford to Old San Juan and the site of the historic Castillo San Juan Felipe del Morro, the fort that guarded entrance into the port of San Juan during Puerto Rico's Spanish period.

A key attraction to Old San Juan was their favorite restaurant, El Jibarito on Calle Del Sol. El Jibarito is an old-style restaurant with truly authentic Puerto Rican flavors. The mofongo (plantains with shrimp) "is to die for." Most Puerto Rican restaurants provided a variety of hot sauces to accompany meals. El Jibarito was a bit unique in that it carried Don Ricardo Pique Sauce, commonly referred to as "The flavors of Puerto Rico in a bottle." As Don Ricardo was a small business operation at the time, few restaurants carried his particular sauce with its rich fruity flavors mixed with plenty of peppers.

Jorge loved to blend his own flavors in a hot sauce. When the waitress came to take drink orders, Jorge would always ask for several hot sauces: Don Ricardo, Pique Verde Boricua (traditional green sauce), Ajilimojili (hot chili peppers), and Walk the Plank Jalapeno Passion sauce (over the top hot). He would then proceed to mix the flavors into his own concoction. This mixture of flavors produced the long-sought-after beads of perspiration on his forehead, a euphoric experience all its own.

Life can be very exciting when love is young. The young couple enjoyed a healthy mixture of work time away from one another and quality time together as a couple, with few worries in the world. It is only natural that as marriage deepens, more energy is consumed in a variety of worries.

Jorge and Mia moved to Texas to enroll in seminary; if Jorge were to pursue a career in ministry, he felt the need for a formal ministry education. As both Mia and Jorge had grown accustomed to ministry being a couple endeavor, both of them enrolled in theological studies and both graduated. These relatively happy educational years produced two children. After graduation, the couple decided to move to Orlando, Florida, with its significant Hispanic population. Jorge found a position as a church pastor and Mia returned to her nursing profession, helping to support the family.

Just when the future seemed to occupy her attention, a phone call opened Mia's past. She received a call from her half-brother, Manuel; she didn't know of a half-brother before the call. It seemed that her father, Angel, wanted Mia to come to New York to spend time with him. Thus, Manuel called on behalf of Mia's father to invite her to New York. Mia took two days off from work to make a long weekend and traveled to Brooklyn, New York, staying in the spare bedroom in her half-brother's home off Bushwick Avenue.

During and after World War II, many Puerto Ricans, and others from Latin America, migrated to Brooklyn and settled in Sunset Park, Red Hook, and Gowanus neighborhoods, all boarding the shipyards where they found employment. Later migrants settled in the Bushwick neighborhood. These neighborhoods became vibrant Latin communities rich with Latin music and culture. The Copacabana Club became a mecca for Latin music and is known widely for the performers who played on the center stage. Other lesser known, but equally important, clubs catered to Latin music culture; these included Freddy's Bar and Backroom and Andalucia Bar and Lounge.

On this trip, Mia learned that her father was an internationally known musician, famous for his guitar and mandolin playing. Her father Angel was in fact Angel Luis Catala. The weekend she was in Brooklyn, her father played for Daniel Santos, who was the featured guest performer at the Copacabana Club. All of this was shocking news for Mia. The shroud of mystery was lifting regarding her father.

Unfortunately, the promise of spending significant time with her father didn't work out as Mia had hoped. Her father's schedule only allowed them a total of four hours together. The highlight of the visit was when her father treated Mia to a fifteen-minute impromptu concert of him playing the guitar for her. Mia remembered his playing as rapturous. She returned home to Orlando with a new appreciation for her father. He was a famous musician, even if he was a poor father, a womanizer, and an alcoholic.

Within a few years of the move to Orlando, Jorge began struggling with inner challenges stemming from his military service; it is hard to unsee what has been seen and experienced. Jorge was diagnosed with post-traumatic stress disorder (PTSD). The night sweats, headaches, and emotional outbursts were heartbreaking to observe. Jorge resigned his pastoral position to focus on getting well, yet he drifted further into a sense of despair. Jorge's downward spiral was hard on Mia and their marriage. After years of struggle, Jorge left the marriage for good. True to his diagnosis, Jorge blamed Mia for the marriage's failure. Though she had supported her husband through hospitalizations and numerous indiscretions, he moved out, robbing Mia of another chance to try to make it work.

Mia threw herself into helping her children make the most of their remaining high school years. She also completed another degree and moved into a teaching position. In spite of disappointments, Mia worked hard to be at the top of her class in her profession and in her responsibilities as a mother.

Then came another phone call from Manuel. In a bit of hysteria, Manuel told Mia that their father was dying. He encouraged Mia to visit and say goodbye to Angel. Apparently, her father was in the final stages of advanced cirrhosis of the liver, brought on by his lifelong abuse of alcohol. Manuel noted their father was in Castaner of all places, staying with his childhood best friend Michael. Apparently, Angel was preforming with Odilio Gonzales at a club in San Juan when he became too ill to perform

Mia made arrangements, and two days later she was in Castaner at her father's bedside. When she arrived, her father was very ill and drifted in and out of consciousness. On the afternoon of the first day, he awoke and immediately recognized Mia. He reached for her face and she leaned forward. With his hands on either side of her face he said, "My little girl, I have always loved you. I am so sorry I wasn't a good father to you." And he began to cry. Mia got out of her chair, sat on the side of the bed, and held her father, soothing him. "I love you too." She held him as he slipped back into unconsciousness. Through most of the night, Mia was either beside his bed or in the bed holding him. She wiped his face with a washcloth or simply held him and stroked his thinning hair.

Early in the morning, Angel's friend Michael tapped on the door and gently opened it. "Ready for some coffee?" he asked. With that he walked in the bedroom with a hot coffee mug and handed it to Mia. She roused her father and helped him get into a half-sitting position. Angel aroused a bit and took a sip of coffee.

For about an hour he was conscious. Mia and Angel talked about his diagnosis. She encouraged him to drink something with lactose in it, like milk. She thought it might help reduce some of the acid in his stomach and the toxicity in his system and thus make him more comfortable. He seemed content to simply continue with the pain medication his doctor had prescribed.

"Castener is such a beautiful, clean, clear slice of life," Angel said, to Mia's surprise.

"I didn't think you liked our little village. It is a small and quaint place," Mia offered.

He replied after a pause, "I didn't leave because of you…or because of your mother. I always have thought of Castener as a 'C Major,' one of the most used chords on the guitar and a very pleasing sound. I left Castener. Castener never left that special place in me."

"So why did you leave?" Mia inquired.

"Why do spindalis mob others?" he replied. (The spindalis is the unofficial bird of Puerto Rico and is known for mobbing, in which a flock of the birds attacks predators.) "It is in their nature."

There was silence. Then Angel continued, "I have always been a restless soul. I can't sit still. I can't stay in one place. The only time I find peace is when I am playing the guitar, the mandolin. Sounding the notes makes me feel part of the music, part of something beautiful."

"I never held it against you, your leaving," said Mia.

"You should have. I let you down. I was a terrible father. A child should be able to depend on her fath—"

Mia interrupted, "I never held it against you. You were being you."

There was a long silence. Angel noted, "Baby, I am really tired. Help me turn a bit." She did, and within a minute he was fast asleep.

Mia wondered what it would have been like to have a father in her life. Never having a father, she had no idea what she had or hadn't missed. Most of the fathers she saw in Castener during her growing-up years were not particularly good examples. She had no idea of what a good or model father would look like; poverty tends to create a hopelessness that pushes everything to the bland and tasteless side of life.

Later, Angel mentioned that his son Manuel was coming to see him, which was news to Mia. He was to arrive at 5:40 A.M. the following day. Angel seemed to be hanging on until his son arrived. He so longed to see him.

That afternoon, Angel woke for a few minutes. Mia had been waiting for the opportunity. She had prepared a cup of milk in hopes that it would reduce his toxicity. "See Papa," she said, "I have *Pitorro* [often referred to as Puerto Rican moonshine] for you." He looked at Mia, smiled, and said, "You are a liar like your father."

It was a long night with chills and restlessness. Mia spent most of the night in the bed with her father. At 5:00 A.M., Angel opened his eyes wide and seemed to know that death was drawing near. He expressed his pride in Mia and again apologized for being such a poor father. Mia responded firmly, "I love you. I forgive you. I was always waiting for you to call. I always understood."

He said, "I don't have long now. I am going to miss you."

"I will treasure our time together over these last days," Mia assured him. "I want to be with you in heaven."

"I would like that very much," her father said. "I am sure you will make it to heaven, but I don't think I belong there."

"Oh, but you do. Getting to heaven isn't about being a perfect person. It is about placing your trust in Jesus Christ. Will you accept him as your Lord and Savior?"

Angel nodded his head and said, "Yes, I will. I accept Jesus—if he will have me. Will you pray for me?"

Holding his hand, Mia began praying. When she finished, Angel simply rested his head more firmly on his pillow. A calm peace seemed to relax his face. He took two more gentle breaths and stopped breathing. It was 5:48 A.M., December 23, 2011.

In the moment he stopped breathing, a low cloud on the horizon moved aside and the room filled with the rush of sunrise light. Mia said in a gentle whisper, "Yes, Jesus, you can take him away." She felt a gentle hand on her shoulder, but she could see no one.

Ten seconds later there was a tapping on the door. It opened gently, and Michael said, "Anyone ready for coffee?" As he opened the door, he saw Mia's face and knew his friend had departed this life.

It was only after her father's death that Mia began to appreciate how accomplished he was in the insular world of Latin music in the seventies, eighties, and nineties. In addition to playing with Daniel Santos, one of the most versatile singers of his generation, Angel Catala played for Bobby Capo, one of the most prolific songwriters in the Spanish-speaking world. His *Piel Canela* was translated into English and French and became the theme for a Mexican movie. Catala toured Mexico, the Caribbean, and South America with Maria Luisa Landrin;

her signature song, "*Amor Perdido*," earned her the title "Queen of the Bolero." She recorded over 150 songs with RCA records. In addition, Catala worked with Tony Aguilar, who recorded over 150 albums, sold over 25 million copies, and acted in over 120 films. In his day, Catala was one of the most sought-after guitarists in the Latin world.

The day after her father's death, Mia left Castaner to catch a flight in San Jaun to go home to Orlando; she wanted to spend Christmas with her own children. Michael planned to take care of the arrangements for Angel's funeral. As Mia drove the winding road leading out of Castaner, she reflected on the journey of her life since she had first traveled this road heading off to college thirty-five years earlier; she had found and lost a husband and a father. At age fifty-three, she wondered what the decades ahead would bring. Thankfully, she had two adult children, both of whom loved her and were supportive. In time, maybe there would be grandchildren as well.

True to who she was, Mia threw herself into her work of educating and training nurses. Like her ancestors before her, Mia found herself strangely alone as she plodded toward an uncertain and challenging future.

Carlos

Arecibo was the perfect location for a modest undercover pirate operation.

The village, and its adjacent river, was named for its Taino chief (cacique), Xamaica Arasibo, who negotiated with Spanish explorers instead of taking up arms to defend the Beloved Island. In this regard Arasibo was an exception. In the early sixteenth century, virtually every other cacique on the island took up arms against the Spanish explorers and did everything possible to resist the cultural changes they tried to enforce.

While Arasibo's accommodation of the Spanish was in stark contrast to the actions of every other cacique, it was very much in keeping with the traditions of his heritage. The village of Arecibo, and Arasibo's family heritage, had always been based on accommodation and compromise. The village was a trading center that attracted people and goods from a large geographical region of coastlines and interior mountain regions of the island. Consequently, it was always a center of cultural diversity with a sharp focus on commerce. Prior to the arrival of Spanish explorers, Arecibo accommodated a vast diversity of traders who bought and sold goods without any interest in knowing the values or morality of those who bought or sold. Commerce was king in Arecibo.

With the coming of the sixteenth century Spanish explorers, and the greatly increased maritime commerce that followed, a local Arecibo fisherman saw an opportunity. Antonio Correa began a makeshift pirate operation using his slow-moving fishing vessel. Later, he and his "mighty crew" managed to steal a small British navy vessel as it lay in harbor at San Juan, 50 miles east of Arecibo; the crew was being entertained in a brothel.

The geography of the area made Arecibo the perfect location for the undercover pirate operation. As the waters of the Arecibo River move northward, approaching the bay of Arecibo, the river makes a sharp turn eastward before letting into the bay. Thus, from a distance a passing ship might not even notice that a river flowed into the bay.

At the broad mouth of the river the water does not run deep. The area appears to be a large marsh with no evidence of a river channel.

Capitan Correa developed a clever strategy for hiding his pirating operation. He would time his arrival and departure at the mouth of the Arecibo River to high tide. At this time, the water level in the hidden Arecibo River was high enough to accommodate a small naval vessel riding high on the tide. Once past the mouth of the river, Correa would position his ship on the westernmost part of the river, hidden behind trees on the river's bank. At that particular location, Correa and his crew dredged the river channel to accommodate his ship to barely float at low tide. The arrangement was brilliant. Typically, Correa's small vessel would arrive and depart at high tide during the night, when Spanish maritime authorities were either asleep or occupied in local bars.

For the better part of three decades, Capitan Correa's pirate operation terrorized small commercial activity on the northern shores of Puerto Rico, especially as vessels went in and out of the San Juan port.

Thus, Arecibo was a town with two distinct personalities: it was known for its cooperation with Spanish overlords, and it was also the center of an economic rebellion against the "invaders." Under the leadership of their Taino cacique, Arasibo, the good people of Arecibo brokered a casual cooperative arrangement with their Spanish overlords. Having seen the destruction of southern tribes as they resisted the Spanish explorers, Arasibo sought a middle way forward for his people.

Even so, among the Good People of the Land of the Noble Lord there simmered a primal urge to sabotage those who disregarded the ancient values of the Taino tradition: simplicity, friendship, openness, kindness, and always peaceful behavior.

The saboteurs, and those who knew of the pirate enterprise, would refer to Arecibo as La Villa del Capitan Correa (Capitan Correa's Villa) or El Diamanté Del Norte (the diamond of the north).

Noting the exception of Capitan Correa, Arecibo was a traditional Taino town in every other regard. For decades before the arrival of Spanish explorers, the town hosted an annual Taino pilgrimage. From all of central Boriken (the pre-Spanish name for the island), pilgrims would come to Arecibo by boat and foot to take the eight-mile pilgrimage to La Cueva del Indio, a cluster of caves with a magnificent view of the Caribbean Sea. It is one of the most beautiful areas on the island. The area features cave drawings dated to AD 1200 and indicate that the site was of religious importance for centuries.

The traditional Taino pilgrims made their journey from Arecibo along the coastline to La Cueva del Indio in conjunction with the winter solstice, arriving at the cave site just as the sun was setting. The night was spent in religious rituals within the cave, and many slept. At sunrise the next morning, the pilgrims began their journey back to Arecibo, concluding the pilgrimage. The days before and after the pilgrimage were feast days in Arecibo, where Taino tribes would gather from the region for council meetings, to trade goods, and to shop prospective brides and grooms who had come of age in the previous year.

The eighteenth and early nineteenth century saw a transition in Arecibo life from its Taino roots and pirate past to the trappings of a bonified municipality. Central to this evolution was the establishment and later construction of the Catedral de San Felipe Apostol (Cathedral of Saint Philip the Apostle); the first modest building, located on a side street, was destroyed in an earthquake in 1787. The new cathedral was completed in 1846. This architecturally impressive building was located in the center of the town between Avenida Jose Diego and Calle Gonzalez Marin and adjacent to the town's central square, Plaza Alcaldia Arecibo. The new location of the cathedral and its imposing size illustrated a significant shift in the cultural perspective of the larger region. The accommodation so characteristic of Arasibo's village was giving way to the stately manner of Spanish invaders.

Interestingly, City Hall was built twenty years later in 1866. As a sign of the changes in Arecibo life, two years after its construction City Hall served as a jail for "revolutionaries" of the El Grito de Lares, the rebellion associated with Lares in 1868. Conversely and with a nod to its past, in 1875 the city officially recognized the Plaza Capitan Correa and Recreational Corridor at the site where Capitan Correa used to anchor his "British" naval vessel.

Maria was born in Arecibo, at home, in 1886; her "birth certificate" noted her birthdate as March 6, 1888—the day her mother took her to the magistrate's office to register. Maria was the first in her family born in Puerto Rico and the last of her progeny to treasure her Spanish heritage.

Maria's ancestors left the plains of Tierra Llana de Huelva, Spain, seeking a better life in the gentle valley of Barranco de Pino on the Canary Island of Isla de Gran Canaria. The original plot of land was divided by the Barranco de Pino a mile before the river flowed into the Barranco de Tenoy and positioned between the villages of Arucas to the west and Cruz del Ovejero to the east. For Maria's distant ancestors, this was their "blessed valley," so named because the Barranco de Pino's headwaters were just below the ancient village of Teror, on the slopes of the island's primary volcanic mountain, Pico de las Nieves. In 1481 a pair of shepherds had seen an apparition of the Virgin Mary on top of a pine tree. Thus, the location became a pilgrim site and later developed into a village with a chapel. By 1590 the town was proclaimed "Villa Mariana." With the completion of the Basilica of Our Lady of the Pine in 1725, the modest town became the religious center of the Canary Islands. Maria's ancestors imagined the river itself carrying blessings from the village of Teror to their plot of land downstream.

The farming enterprise grew substantially over several generations. In time, Maria's ancestors became reasonably wealthy in their sugarcane farming operation. By the mid-nineteenth century, sugar exports from the Canary Islands peaked due to the growing sugar production of the Caribbean Islands. The Caribbean Islands quickly became the talk of the Canary Island sugarcane farmers. Some sought to organize a cooperative to combat the loss of market share.

Others saw a rare opportunity. Maria's grandfather was one of them; he sold his sugarcane operation in the Canary Islands and headed to Arecibo, Puerto Rico, with his wife and two sons. There he bought land south and southwest of the village of Arecibo for the beginning of his sugar plantation dream.

Hugo, one of the young boys who settled in the Arecibo area, later became Maria's father. By the time of Maria's birth, the family was established as one of the leading families of the growing Arecibo region. The farming operation easily supported the extended family. In addition to sugarcane, the family grew tobacco and a variety of vegetables. As a way of expanding the family's business operation, Hugo and his wife moved into the village of Arecibo and established a grocery store. Initially, the couple lived in the back room of the store. After several years, they purchased a home two blocks away on the town's main street, Avenida Jose de Diego, just west of the intersection with Calle Palma. This is the house where Maria was born the next year, 1886.

While Maria was the first of her family born in Puerto Rico, she was arguably the most Spanish of the entire family. She took great pride in her Spanish roots. The music, history, culture, art, and poetry of her heritage were her lifelong passion. Part of Maria's passion was native to her spirit, her disposition; even so, the changing circumstances of her life also played a major role in solidifying her passion for all things Spanish. Maria was born into a cauldron of change. As she was transitioning from child to woman, Puerto Rico was transitioning from Spanish to American.

Prior to Maria's birth, the Lares rebellion of 1868 was a symptom of the growing unrest of the people of Puerto Rico with the ruling Spanish. At the time of Maria's birth, the government of Puerto Rico was moving out from under Spanish rule toward autonomy. The Autonomic Charter approved in 1897 allowed Puerto Rico proportional representation in Spain and at home. The first autonomous cabinet was formed in February 1898, and the first legislative elections were held a month later in March 1898. This rapid march toward independence was halted in April 1898 when the United States declared war on Spain. All legislative deliberations abruptly ended on July 25 when the United States invaded Puerto Rico. The long and tortuous road toward autonomy ended with Puerto Rico becoming a "possession," later a territory, of the United States.

The path from "Spanish to autonomy to American possession" was a rollercoaster of disaster for many in Puerto Rico. This political transition impacted Maria's family in two primary ways. First, the American invasion created great social instability as average Puerto Ricans saw an opportunity to disregard the past and create a fresh and new beginning for themselves. Much of agricultural production in Puerto Rico at the time was built around a hacienda model for farming. A wealthy farmer (the hacienda owner) would collaborate with numerous small family farms in the surrounding area to move product to market. The hacienda owner served as the banker for the smaller farmers in the area, offering them loans to buy seed for planting; these loans were typically paid off when the harvest was sold. Over decades, and after more than a few bad growing seasons, the debts of the small farmers increased. This arrangement meant that some small, poorly run farms were in constant debt and in danger of being taken over by their creditors.

With the US invasion, large numbers of small farmers began organizing themselves into "partidas"—groups of forty to one hundred men who descended on haciendas and commercial establishments to loot and destroy all financial records, including all records of what small farmers owed to the "haciendas." The destroying of debt records meant that Maria's extended family lost thousands upon thousands of pesos.

Second, once Puerto Rico was occupied, the military governor (a United States general) altered the exchange rate between the US dollar and the Puerto Rican peso. This was done to create an incentive for large US corporations to invest in Puerto Rico. Changing the exchange rate was devastating for Maria's family: it was far easier to sell devaluated property to US corporations like Domino (sugar company) than to navigate the economic tsunami unfolding in Puerto Rico. What Maria's extended family didn't lose to the "partidas" or the reevaluation of the peso, they lost in the Great Depression twenty-five years later. The only family asset that survived was the small grocery store in Arecibo.

In the midst of heartbreaking financial reversals, Maria loved to quote Spanish poetry from the Classical Period. When so much was going so wrong in her life, she clung to her Spanish heritage and remembered the grandeur that once was.

Carlos remembered his grandmother Maria as an intelligent, quirky woman. While she could quote Spanish poetry and sing Spanish folk songs with perfect annunciation, she was distrustful of local Catholic (Spanish) priests and was a critic of virtually everything in Puerto Rican culture of the time. Maria had little use for the local priest, yet she daily offered prayers in a corner of her living room where she kept a statue of St. Antony of Padua (Italian Sant'Antonio di Padova), the patron saint of the poor. Carlos saw great irony in the fact that his grandmother enjoyed singing Spanish ballads (originally performed 300 years before in Spanish State events with dancing) but was opposed to Carlos attending local parties and dances reflecting the emerging traditions of Puerto Rico. Maria was selective in her appreciation of music.

After his grandfather died (at forty-two years old from a head injury), Carlos's family moved in with Maria; Carlos's father insisted that he wanted to take care of Maria, and there was no way she would leave her little "palace" on Avenida Jose de Diego. This house where Carlos grew up was not much of a palace; it was a small home with three small eight-by-ten-foot bedrooms and no closets. In the late 1950s and early 1960s, Carlos's house was the only remaining residence on the block. Long before, residents had sold their modest homes to make room for commercial establishments: a tattoo parlor, a TV repair shop, a shoe repair shop, a consignment shop, a barber, a pawn shop, and two bars.

Carlos remembered playing many street games in his childhood: hide and seek was a standard with a few improvisations. The game was started with someone throwing a broomstick. The person who was "it" had to run and retrieve the stick while others ran to hide. Once caught, children had to wait at the streetlight for another child to free them with a touch. Other childhood games included "I Got You Last," jump rope with a hundred variations, marbles, and spinning tops. With spinning tops, the object of the game was to knock your opponent's top out of the circle. In Carlos's neighborhood, children developed a variation of the game where the metal point of the top was sharpened; when you threw your top into the circle you tried to land it on top of an opponent's top, bursting it apart as the sharpened metal point served as a wedge. Carlos's mother took a dim view of this variation of the game and scolded Carlos when she learned he had been playing it. "That is very dangerous," she said. "Someone is going to take out an eye with that foolishness. If you lose an eye, when you get home, I am going to take out the other one." The danger was not theoretical; on one occasion a sharpened top flew out of the circle, leaving an inch-long slash in the top of Carlos's head. Carlos was taken to a friend's house, where he begged his friends not to tell his mother. As the cut was covered by hair, Carlos's mother never found out about the injury until decades later when he confessed to her.

Another favorite endeavor for Arecibo boys was unsupervised swimming in the ocean, which was strictly forbidden. The group would hide swimming trunks under the bleachers at school. After school, they would go under the bleachers and change into their trunks and head out the two blocks to the ocean. After an enjoyable swim they would change clothes under the bleachers, leave their trunks to dry, and head home. This became a near daily routine.

As an older child, aged ten to twelve, Carlos and his mother took summer trips to New York. Carlos had four uncles living in New York; they had all relocated from Puerto Rico seeking employment opportunities. Carlos and his mother typically stayed with Uncle Louis, who lived on East 108th Street in Manhattan, next to a large open-air market for Latinos. Originally, this northernmost Upper East Side neighborhood had consisted primarily of working-class immigrants from Ireland, Germany, and Italy. This gave way to an influx of Southern Italians and Sicilians. In the early twentieth century, the area was known as Italian Harlem and was the founding location of the Genovese crime family, one of the Five Families that dominated organized crime in New York City.

After WWI, Puerto Rican migrants established an enclave around Lexington Avenue between 105th Street and 112th Street. By the mid-twentieth century, the neighborhood increasingly became Latino as the growth of Puerto Ricans pushed up into what was historically known as East Harlem. In time, the area was referred to as Spanish Harlem or simply El Barrio ("The Neighborhood").

Carlos remembered meeting his uncle Thomas. Thomas had migrated to New York City much earlier than his brothers, so Carlos had no memory of meeting him in Puerto Rico. Getting to see Thomas was always a convoluted process that involved meeting a third party outside a bar, proof of identity, and a ride in the back of a windowless van. Meeting with Thomas was a brief affair of ten to fifteen minutes. In addition, he was always surrounded by a small crowd of men. Carlos thought of Uncle Thomas as a distracted, distant, cold soul. Thomas was an underworld figure. As the population of Puerto Ricans increased, entrepreneurs like Thomas worked their way into the lower echelons of the Genovese crime family. While Thomas remained below the radar in terms of media coverage, he did appear in the last known photo of acting boss Antony "Tony Bender" Strollo immediately prior to Strollo's mysterious disappearance (boss Vito "Don Vito" Genovese was in prison at the time). In the *New York Times* front-page photo, Thomas was the slightly out-of-focus unidentified man looking out the café window as Strollo was hustled into a waiting car.

Carlos also remembered the fire hydrant episode; he and his cousin were walking down East 110th Street when a neighborhood troublemaker opened a fire hydrant on them. Both boys lost their footing and were shoved off the sidewalk by the force of gushing water. There were no fire hydrants to worry about in Puerto Rico.

Carlos embraced and enjoyed his trips to New York City. Maybe the most important aspect of the trips was that they gave the "boy from Arecibo" an expanded framework for understanding people and the culture they espoused. In the grand melting pot of El Barrio, Carlos interacted with people, especially children, from a host of countries: Cuba, Grenada, Dominion Republic, Italy, Spain, Portugal, Brazil, Argentina, Mexico, and a few old-timers from Germany. The boy who grew up on fish tacos delighted in pizza, feijoada, dulce de leche, provoleta, and rotis, but not so much in sauerkraut.

Standing in front of the Empire State Building made it hard for him to think of Arecibo City Hall in the same way. Arecibo friends were always interested to hear of Carlos's adventures in New York City. Neighborhood friends in Arecibo just couldn't get enough information about Carlos's travels. So he would describe in great detail what it was like to fly in an airplane, walk the streets of El Barrio, eat the foods of other nations, and play new street games.

Of course, his Arecibo friends sometimes had trouble believing what he reported about his trips. His description of the Empire State Building didn't go over so well with his friend Evita, who didn't believe it was possible to build a 102-story building. "It would fall over," she said. Any number of friends kept asking about foreign languages Carlos claimed to have heard on his trip. One year, Carlos came back with a rather poor pronunciation of a foreign phrase to impress his friends: "Küss meinen Hintern."

Two blocks away from where Carlos would stay in New York lived an old German couple, the brunt of much laughter among Carlos's cousins. Once, Carlos asked the old man for a German phrase he could use to impress the girls back in Arecibo.

The old man thought for a moment and said, "Küss meinen Hintern."

"What does it mean in English?" Carlos asked.

"Oh, you are going to like this," the old man said. "It means 'you are lovely.'"

Carlos was impressed. Upon his return, Carlos spoke the phrase to a few of his heartthrobs. The reaction was always the same.

"What did you say?" the girl would ask.

"It is German," he would reply.

"What does it mean?"

"It means, 'you are lovely.'" The girls would always blush. They were also impressed that such a traveled young man could speak a little German along with Spanish and English.

It was many years later when Carlos learned that the old German had the last laugh. "Küss meinen Hintern" doesn't translate as "you are lovely" but rather as "kiss my butt." Apparently, the old German had grown tired of children laughing at him and his noble tradition.

In the summer when Carlos was fifteen, his uncle Ray made him an offer too good to turn down. Ray, who had moved from Manhattan to Central Florida to find work with the expanding Disney enterprise (Walt Disney World), suggested that Carlos move to Orlando for the summer. Carlos did, and he never returned to live in Puerto Rico.

With the move to Orlando (Altamont Springs), Carlos began attending a Seventh-day Adventist church with his uncle Ray. His attendance wasn't really voluntary. In Adventist thinking, if anyone living in the house did not attend the church's meetings, it reflected badly on the head of the house. Attending a church service or two was easy for him to accept as the price to live in Florida.

Carlos met Angela, his future wife, at Forest Lake Academy, attached to the Forest Lake Seventh-day Adventist Church on East Semoran Blvd. They dated for five years before they married in 1977. Thereafter, they headed off to college at Southern Adventist University in Collegedale, Tennessee (east of Chattanooga), where Angela was an education major and he majored in religion. After their graduations in 1981, the couple returned to Central Florida seeking employment. Angela was offered a job at Gateway Christian School in Mount Dora, attached to the Mount Dora Seventh-day Adventist Church. Within a few months, Carlos was offered a job as a ministerial assistant at the church. At the time, Mount Dora was a modest, sleepy town with a population of less than 6,000.

In those days, Elijah Venden was the pastor of the Mount Dora SDA church. He was a well-known preacher in SDA circles and one of the pioneers of TV ministries among the SDA brethren. Initially, Carlos was responsible for up-linking the TV ministry to a rented satellite that broadcast to a variety of media outlets. This meant the Mount Dora service, attended by 350 people, was broadcast literally around the world to SDA churches. Part of the attraction to Venden's ministry was the modest size of his church. People who watched the TV programs thought of Venden as "one of us." He wasn't a celebrity. He lived in a world like that of his listeners.

As the ministry grew, largely because of the TV ministry, Venden developed a busy schedule speaking at numerous SDA camp meetings around the country: Wichita, Kansas; Aspen, Colorado; Concord, New Hampshire; Pierre, South Dakota; Bismark, North Dakota; and Loma Linda, California. Carlos traveled with Venden, as he was the person with the skills to upload to the satellite. With this increased activity, Carlos began taking on more responsibility, including occasionally preaching or leading one of Venden's workshops. With his varied background, Carlos was a natural fit for an expanding role in Venden's growing ministry.

Even so, for Carlos there were some challenges working with Venden and the SDA theological framework at the time. Seventh-day Adventists are known for three prominent characteristics: they worship on Saturday, are strict vegetarians, and project a strong focus on health care. Their hospitals are sprinkled around the country and provide first-rate health care; the best known may be Loma Linda University's Medical Center.

Ellen White was the co-founder of the Seventh-day Adventist Church, along with Joseph Bates and her husband James White. White had a series of visions beginning in 1844 and continuing until 1863. Her visions, and the books that flowed from them (forty-plus), served as theological and practical foundation stones for SDA churches. Maybe the most unique feature of SDA theology centers on its understanding of the Heavenly Sanctuary and Investigative Judgment.

The Jewish Temple of Solomon's time was divided into three sections. The first was open to male worshippers. The second area, the Holy Place, was where the priest intervened with God on behalf of the worshippers every Sabbath. The third area was the Most Holy Place (Holy of Holies) where the priest, only entering once a year, intervened on behalf of the people. Based on several Old Testament and New Testament texts, SDA theology suggests that the atoning work of Christ is also divided into three aspects. After his death and resurrection, Jesus went into the Holy Place in the Heavenly Sanctuary to intervene on behalf of people. In 1844 (the year of White's first vision), Christ entered the Most Holy Place in the Heavenly Sanctuary to continue to intervene on behalf of believers. The Investigative Judgment doctrine suggests that every person who has ever lived, and every aspect of his/her life, is judged in the Heavenly Sanctuary to determine if they have lived in accordance to God's commands and may go into heaven.

While the details of this theological framework are challenging to those new to SDA theology, grasping a sense of it is important. As American culture became more secular in the mid- to late-twentieth century, more progressive views began to creep into SDA life, as also happened with Methodists, Presbyterians, Baptists, and virtually every church in the US.

As with the history of other religious bodies, the slow-moving SDA challenges embodied themselves in a particular person and time: Desmond Ford and the "Sanctuary Review Committee" that met with him at Glacier View Ranch near Denver, Colorado, in August 1980. In the previous year, Dr. Ford delivered a lecture suggesting there was no biblical basis for the SDA doctrine of the Heavenly Sanctuary or the Investigative Judgment, both essential and foundational beliefs of SDA churches. The result of the Glacier View Ranch meeting was that Ford was fired as an SDA professor. While the committee's decision brought an end to the immediate issue—Dr. Ford—the larger issue continued to stew in the SDA community.

Traditional versus progressive voices in the SDA continued to pull and tug at the fabric of the SDA church. Carlos tended to side with the more progressive wing of the struggle, while Elijah Venden was a staunch traditionalist. Carlos wanted to rely on scripture more than the visions and writings of Ellen White. He wanted to see the church's worship modernized. For Carlos, all of this was more than a theoretical matter; his employer was on the other side of the aisle! As he learned in the coming years, his wife Angela was also on the traditional side of the struggle. In time, the denominational struggle became a family struggle.

Reports from the Glacier View Ranch meeting and its "resolution" quickly began circulating among SDA clergy. Laity learned about it much more slowly. At first, most traditional SDA church attenders appreciated the clarity: traditional values were reaffirmed. Then those same traditional church attenders became surprised that so many in their local churches were displeased with the "resolution." As with all denominational groups in the US at the time, the progressive-traditional divisions were much deeper than originally imagined.

Soon, the Mount Dora congregation was buzzing with conversation. Some in the church were pleased with the resolution, and others were not. The conversation among laity in the SDA church wasn't really about biblical or theological nuances; it was about embracing more contemporary music in worship, relaxing some dietary restrictions, and expanding the role of women in the church. For clergy it was a different and deeper conversation: in terms of authority, they wondered, do we place more emphasis on the teachings of Ellen White or on the Bible?

This debate in the Mount Dora church became significant. It was so significant, in fact, that the Rev. Venden addressed it in a sermon broadcast through his TV ministry. To his critics, it became known as the "soft sermon." In his sermon, Verden attempted to soften the immediate impact of the Glacier View Ranch resolution while remaining a staunch traditionalist. This approach went over well with his widespread international audience, as most of those churches were strong traditionalists. It went over poorly with a large segment of his Central Florida church members. The "soft sermon" changed the conversation within the Mount Dora congregation from "What shall we do?" to "When shall some of us pull out and start a new church?"

Eventually, ninety-six members of the Mount Dora church left to start a new SDA congregation. Once constituted, the new church leaders began recruiting Carlos as their pastor. Carlos and Angela wrestled with what to do. In the end, Carlos accepted the position; Angela was hesitant but embraced the decision, as Carlos was acting in his head-of-the-house role in Adventist ways of thinking.

Things rarely work out as well as we initially hope: Angela came under a lot of pressure from her parents, who were staunch traditionalists; the original ninety-six members found starting a new church much harder than they had thought; and the SDA hierarchy made it difficult for the new church to easily become an official SDA congregation on any reasonable timeline.

After twenty-five years of marriage and three children, Carlos and Angela parted ways. Each had a list of annoying habits of the other, as in every marriage, but the foundational issue that ate at the essence of the relationship was the progressive-traditional divide. Angela had been reared in a hyper-traditional SDA family, while Carlos had a diversified religious background and came late to SDA traditions. In the rapidly changing world of the early twenty-first century, Angela sought stability and meaning in the Adventist faith of her parents and grandparents. Carlos, on the other hand, embraced change and diversity at every turn: he was a native of Arecibo and loved the diversity of New York City, Orlando, and Tennessee. It was Carlos who first uttered the words, "This isn't working for either of us. We are not happy and things are not going to get better for us. We should go our separate ways and find more promising new beginnings."

Carlos paid dearly for his new beginning. In addition to losing a wife, he lost a career.

For income, Carlos fell back on a talent he had picked up in Arecibo. He went back to cutting hair. In Puerto Rico, Carlos had cut his friends' hair as a way of making a few extra paseos. After his divorce, he imagined that he would barber until he could figure out what he wanted to do long term. He enjoyed the cosmetology work and the stability it provided, so he just kept doing it. He was good at it and it provided steady income after his divorce.

In addition, this work allowed Carlos to fulfill his calling in ministry. In Central Florida at the time, the barber shop was a hub of the Latino community, especially for men. Men from all walks of life frequented the shop and shared their challenges and joys as they sat in Carlos's therapeutic and healing chair; and they got a great haircut to boot. Due to his diverse experience and ministry training, Carlos was a barber like no other.

On a personal level, this was also a season of extended reflection and self-examination for Carlos. The "boy from Arecibo" began thinking about himself and his life journey in new and deeper ways. The impetus for this deeper journey came in a casual comment a client made to him. The client was originally from El Paraiso, a small village outside Ponce, Puerto Rico. He was career military and had traveled all over the world. He had the most interesting and fascinating stories one could imagine. As he was leaving the shop one day, after an affectionate conversation with Carlos about their homeland, he made an offhand comment: "You never get over where you were born."

The words resonated in the deep places of Carlos's soul. With the help of a psychologist, Carlos began an inner journey of discovery and understanding. The psychologist challenged Carlos to think about the values he cherished as "voices" from prominent people in his past—his parents, his uncles, his friends—and from his birthplace, Arecibo. One of the most prominent voices from his past was his grandmother, Maria. Hers was a delightful but also conflicted voice. In the midst of rapid cultural changes in her day, Maria never was able to make peace with those changes; thus, she harshly critiqued everything Puerto Rican—not just in her day but in her grandson Carlos as well.

Carlos's counseling relationship with the psychologist lasted less than six months, but the insights he gained in the process continued to serve him well for years. On his own timeframe he began unpacking psychological baggage from the past and experienced a new, healthier, and happier sense of himself.

Instead of seeing himself as a divorced man in transition, he saw himself as a happy man with an incredibly well-suited job that he loved. His cosmetology work was going well, providing more than enough to support himself, *and* he loved the quality relationships he was developing in the larger Central Florida Latino community. He wasn't just the guy who cuts your hair; he was an advisor, a life coach, a mentor, a role model, a sage full of wisdom and spiritual insight. Having discovered the place where he belonged while so many others continued the search was liberating to Carlos. He settled into his career.

Through the divorce, Carlos retained his relationships with his three adult children. During their growing-up years, Carlos had always been an attentive father. He was easygoing, loved to play, and thought the world of his children. At family gatherings Carlos was the adult running around outside with the children while Angela and others sat around talking about the troubles in the world and articulating the rules that should be followed to correct the situation.

Carlos's inward journey and liberation also led him to a new activity—dance. Denied the opportunity to explore dance as a child and teenager, Carlos enrolled in a dance class. Later he referred to dance as "my rebellion."

It was at the Pulse Dance Studio (PDS) that Carlos tried salsa for the first time, and oh did he like it! Salsa became for him a kind of active therapy. He took every salsa class the local studio offered. It wasn't about the dance partner, the music, or the location; it was a joyful celebration of his Puerto Rican heritage. It was a celebration of what it meant to be from Arecibo and to live in the Latino community of Central Florida. As a complete surprise to him, Carlos became a very good dancer and eventually served as one of the studio's best-loved dance teachers.

Carlos developed a rather interesting approach to teaching dance. Most instructors tended to begin teaching steps with a dance pair. That is, a couple would come for dance lessons, and the instructor would teach them to dance as a couple, the man leading and the woman following. Carlos taught individuals to dance solo, on their own. Once the individuals learned the steps and could do them intuitively, he then put the students in pairs. This unique approach was an outgrowth of Carlos's own journey. For him dance was about joy, freedom, and celebration. Salsa was a favorite dance form for Carlos because it was easily adapted to one's personal style and one's momentary emotions and feelings. Teaching dance as an individual activity allowed greater freedom of expression for students and helped them identify what they liked most about dance movement.

The challenge for Carlos's style of teaching was to pair up couples after each individual discovered their own unique dance style. The eventual dance pairing required a few adjustments: the man had to learn how to lead and the woman had to learn how to read the man's cues for dance moves; and then each had to learn to dance with another person in "their space." While Carlos had a strong argument for his "individual first" teaching method, he developed the style out of his commitment to dance as an expression of inner feelings and emotions.

For the "boy from Arecibo," dance was first and foremost therapy.

People enroll in dance classes for a variety of reasons. Some couples simply want to get better at dancing together. Others want to prepare for an upcoming wedding reception or high school reunion. Many come to dance classes as a stepping stone to meeting a new person.

Carlos became adept at figuring out a person's overall objective in coming to dance class. The "finding a new someone" crowd was easy to spot; they usually enrolled as a small group of women or a solo man. While Carlos enjoyed teaching anyone to dance, he had a particular preference for couples who came wanting to learn to dance better together. Having lost a life partner, Carlos seemed especially committed to helping couples learn to find joy and delight in embracing their unique dance styles. After all, the couple that dances together stays together!

Carlos was always surprised when a woman who came to dance class to "find a new someone" showed interest in him. He was pleased that PDS had a strict policy against instructors fraternizing with students. This allowed him to keep his distance; he wasn't ready to engage in another relationship. Dance was his therapy, not a way to find a new someone.

Carlos and Mia

In his 2021 album *Salsa: The Rhythm of Passion*, the noted songwriter and composer Gianluigi Toso collected some of the best-known salsa songs into one compilation. He also identified a characteristic often associated with salsa music: passion.

In its most basic form, salsa is known for its three quick steps in four beats, rotating hips, and different accompanying instruments emphasizing even or odd beats. The odd number of steps and the varied instrumental emphases on odd and even beats create an inherent syncopation to salsa dancing. They also provide for a complex multitude of individual dance moves, allowing dancers to develop unique styles within the salsa genre.

The food salsa originated with natives in South America who domesticated the tomato. By the 1500s, when Spanish adventurers first encountered the "sauce," it was used widely in the Caribbean. The term "salsa" in Spanish quickly took on the sense of spicy hot.

In the musical context, the term "salsa" might be yelled out in a concert to encourage the musicians to play faster and livelier. Much of Cuban music in the 1950s might be described as salsa, but it was in the context of the Latin music scene in 1970s New York City that the term was coined to refer to a specific style of Latin music. The roots of salsa music and dance were certainly Cuban, but what the genre became in the diaspora of New York City was something far trendier and more complex.

Like the making of a complex quilt, salsa pulled from a variety of traditions from Spanish, African, and Caribbean roots into a system easily adapted to individual tastes and open to new possibilities. Rooted in the Caribbean soil of their births, salsa brought together Mia and Carlos.

Mia found navigating the waters of separation and possible divorce to be profoundly difficult. In the first place, she never wanted to be separated or a divorcée. Second, she was desperately afraid that she would become the angry person her mother had become because of her father's failures. In the midst of her fears, loss, and loneliness, Mia sought to forge a way forward where she could continue to be herself and find fulfillment and joy in life. Her children moving forward into adulthood added complexity to her journey. While she wanted them to find their own futures in college and beyond, she still missed the daily role of being their mother. They had become independent adults. Every parent hopes for this, but it brought an unexpected added loneliness to Mia's spirit.

Mia's struggles tended to be more of the sad and chronic type as opposed to the acute or disabling type. Thus, she bravely plodded along, continuing to excel at work and in the volunteer projects she embraced. Even so, a sense of sadness seemed to permeate every aspect of her day.

Mia's coworker Anne befriended her during her separation journey. Anne had traveled a similar path a full decade before Mia and couldn't help but take an interest in her. One day Anne announced, "Enough of the gloom and despair. You're divorced. So what! We are going dancing!"

Mia was horrified. "I am not going out. I am not interested in a man in my life."

"Who said anything about a man? We both know men are unreliable and not worth the effort," Anne replied with enthusiasm.

They both laughed, as "unreliable" and "not worth the effort" had become sarcastic phrases the two often used as they joked about men and their sense of loss. They both shared the conviction that "men make life too complex." At this point in their lives, neither was interested in romance of any kind.

Mia told Anne, "I am just not ready to move forward and look for another relationship."

"Well," Anne said, "let me know when you change your mind."

Mia saw no reason to change her mind.

Several months later, Mia sat in her regular place in worship at the Joyful Baptist Church. That Sunday the pastor's sermon was on "staying the course." He challenged his listeners to focus on doing the right thing and then stick to it regardless of the cost. As Mia thought about the sermon in the following week, she attempted to see if there was truth in it for her. She began to wonder if "sticking to it" was an encouragement for her to remain separated but not legally divorced. She made an appointment to see the pastor in his office.

As she sat in the pastor's office, she brought him up to date on her separation. The pastor was surprised to learn that Mia put off the divorce proceedings; she had been separated and in an unhappy marriage for the better part of five years.

She tried to explain. "In your sermon you encouraged us all to do the right thing and to keep doing it. I have tried to do the right thing for my children. Though they are grown and out of the house, I want to model for them a committed marriage and not just running from marital problems. I want to show them that commitment to marriage is important and you don't just give up when it is hard."

The pastor thought for a long second. He had known the struggles Mia and Jorge had faced. He had talked with Jorge on several occasions and knew his significant challenges. He also knew it was impossible to salvage the relationship. He said to Mia, "You have shown your children what it means to be committed to marriage. Now, you need to show them how to move forward with dignity and grace. It is time, Mia." While it was only pastoral advice, for Mia his words seemed to resound with heavenly thunder. The pastor said out loud what Mia had felt in the deepest places of her spirit. She simply needed someone she respected to say the words.

It is a liberating moment when you realize you are done—that moment when you have crawled forward up a steep, rocky hill to save something and you come to the moment when you realize, "I am done with this foolishness. I am not doing this anymore. It is no way forward for me. I am done."

Mia left the pastor's office and walked across the parking lot to her car with a more purposeful step. Like Aixa her ancestor, Mia set her gaze on a new future.

Anne was delighted to learn that Mia was *finally* interested in a dance class. The two "sisters" decided to help one another back toward a normal life. Anne's friend recommended dance classes at Pulse.

The two enrolled and began attending the weekly classes. These turned into dancing two nights a week, and then occasional weekends were added.

Six months into their shared dancing enterprise, Mia and Anne ended up in a class taught by Carlos. It wasn't long before the three became friends.

By its nature, dancing requires that someone lead and someone follow, else everything settles into a mishmash of confusion. The man leads and the woman follows. Sometimes the woman finds the sequences of moves convoluted and disjointed. Sometimes the woman finds the sequences easy and natural. And sometimes the leading is like a subtle suggestion enthusiastically embraced by the woman.

Carlos had learned that while he technically "led" the dance, it was really the woman's disposition that set the parameters. If the woman was new to dancing and hesitant, then Carlos would lead firmly and stick to basic steps—no spontaneous improvising with a cautious woman. On the other hand, if the woman was confident, a great dancer, and able to quickly adjust to dance cues, then the dance became an adventure.

Anne was like most of the students Carlos had taught through the years; she wanted to learn to be a better dancer *and* stay in complete control of herself and every movement. For Anne, there was no going with the flow or losing herself in the music. From a very early age, Anne had learned that bad things happen when she is not in control. Consequently, her dancing style was controlled, predictable, and contained, which meant that she and salsa were a bit of an oxymoron.

Mia's dancing style was initially guarded, defensive, protective. As Mia had a long history of going to the gym two to three times a week or more, she was trim, firm, and muscular. The "message" Carlos got from Mia during their first dance as instructor and student was, "You don't want to upset me."

As the trio shared meals, went places together, and expressed past heartaches, they became trusted friends. Even so, this changed nothing for Anne's dancing style; after all, bad things happen when you lose control. Mia was different in this regard; with trusted friends she lowered her defenses and gushed warmth, laughter, emotion, and outward expressions of affection. While Anne's life lesson was to stay in control, Mia's was "I am going to be myself and let the chips fall where they may." The disappointment of her divorce had pretty much eclipsed Mia's sense of self. She had gone into a temporary protective mode. Salsa, especially with Carlos, freed up something in Mia so she could again be herself.

Anne noticed the difference in Mia and in the way she danced with Carlos.

One evening, Anne and Mia met for a quick dinner before dance class. Toward the end of the meal Anne said, "Mia, I am not going to dance class tonight."

"Why not?" Mia asked.

"Because the bicycle doesn't need a third wheel," came Anne's reply.

Mia was startled. She didn't realize her good friend had sensed that Mia's feelings for Carlos had moved beyond friendship. Mia wondered if Carlos's feelings towards her were possibly moving into romantic territory, but she had not shared those thoughts with Anne.

Anne laughed. She said, "Mia, I am really happy for you. I am glad you are interested in Carlos. I think you two would be wonderful for each other."

Mia felt immediate anxiety. She felt exposed that Anne had so clearly identified Mia's private feelings and thoughts. She was afraid the situation was quickly moving into new and unfamiliar emotional territory. She innocently asked, "Do you think Carlos might be interested in me?"

Anne laughed loudly and said, "Carlos, gentleman that he is, has been patiently waiting for you to figure this out for some time. He is very interested in you. He doesn't want to ruin a friendship with you by approaching you before you are ready for a dating relationship."

Mia sat dumbfounded. She couldn't deny anything Anne had said.

Later, she sat in her car in the parking lot outside the dance studio. She couldn't go inside without Anne, else everyone in the class would ask where Anne was. She was also hesitant fully to embrace the reality that she was romantically interested in Carlos. Five minutes after the class started, Mia walked in. As everyone was dancing, no one asked about Anne until the midway break. As the instructor, Carlos always made it a point to dance at least once with each of the female students. Sensing Mia was not her normal self, distracted and nervous, he purposely avoided dancing with her. For the last dance of the class he casually walked to Mia, extended his hand, and asked, "Might I have this dance, señorita?"

Mia forced a fearful smile and extended a trembling hand.

Music can be a delightful conversation without words. So it was for Mia and Carlos. This particular dance began with muscular tension and a measure of caution on Mia's part. There isn't much inhibited in salsa; the two friends eventually went with the music and ended the dance in the easy, natural flow of the music.

They smiled at one another. Carlos noted there was a dance scheduled for the Latino Community Center for Friday night and asked, "Will you go with me?"

Without batting an eye, Mia calmly replied, "Yes, pick me up at seven."

In the days, weeks, and years that followed (an entire decade actually), Carlos was patient. Mia was cautious. In the end, salsa won.

On Carlos's side of the equation, he let his friends know early on that he had a "first date on Friday night." His friends and clients were overjoyed to learn about this new date and the prospects of a new beginning for the man who had been so encouraging to so many over the years. For Carlos's friends, this was good news too long in coming.

On Mia's side of the equation, there was mostly silence. She didn't share the news about a new man in her life for weeks. Even so, her close friends knew something was up; Mia was unusually quiet and there seemed to be a glow about her. When she asked if she could "bring a friend" to a picnic, her friend on the other end of the phone line replied, "Well, of course. That would be very nice."

The picnic crowd fell in love with Carlos from the first "hello." This small circle of friends had walked with Mia through the terrible pain of a failed marriage and had been praying and pulling for her to rise above the disappointment. As only the dearest of friends could do, they blessed her "new friend" with opened arms and hearts.

As Carlos began showing up in the larger circle of Mia's friends, it almost became comical; people waited discreetly before rushing over to meet him. And then there was the one Sunday when a handsome Latino man sat alone in the small congregation at the Joyful Baptist Church. Longtime members sat in their regular seats and cut eyes back and forth to other old friends, silently questioning who this man was. As the Sunday school classes dismissed and people began coming into the chapel for worship, others noticed this man and assumed he was simply a first-time visitor.

Then Mia walked in with the Sunday school crowd, chatting with a friend. As they ended the conversation, Mia walked up the aisle, turned into the pew, and sat next to Carlos. Almost in unison, smiles broke out on every face around the little chapel, as if the worshippers were listening to a particularly moving silent rendition of Handel's "Hallelujah Chorus." It was a particularly good day in church. It was one of those Sundays when "Good News" had already been proclaimed before the pastor rose to deliver the sermon.

Baptist congregations can be the strangest of assemblies. Baptists are fiercely independent in their thinking. A long historic mantra of Baptist is "We agree to disagree agreeably." And, more or less, Baptists tend to live into that hope. They certainly do live fully into the "disagree" aspect of the mantra. Baptist bodies are very democratic, and one person equals one vote, even if the voter has no idea what is being voted on—which is sometimes the case. Baptists are known to allow disagreements to fester and eventually split a church, with one group going down the road a half mile and starting a new church.

Even with all their challenges, Baptists can come together in unbelievable unity when they feel something is "of God," when they sense in the deepest places of the heart that something is "just right." So the little band of Joyful Baptists smiled ear to ear and came together in support of Mia and her new fellow.

Carlos had been sitting with Mia in worship for nearly five years when people began wondering if the pair had married. Mia confirmed that they were not married. Two Sundays later, eighty-five-year-old

Miss Bessy made it her business to go over and talk to Carlos before Sunday school let out and Mia made her way into the chapel.

No one ever accused Miss Bessy of being shy, indirect, or savvy. She pretty much demanded that Carlos explain why he wasn't willing to marry Mia. Every time Carlos started to offer a reply, Missy Bessy would say, "Don't you interrupt this poor old lady." With that she would keep pressuring him. Finally, Carlos spit out the truth: "I've asked her several times. She is the one who wants to wait."

With that Miss Bessy offered a confused, "Oh, I see." Creaking, she got up and went back to her regular seat.

Mia listened pretty much for four years as friends, her children, and extended family members encouraged her to say "yes."

Sara

Sima Abajian and Yesnich Hagopian met on Ellis Island; both were refugees in a wave of immigration to the United States in the early twentieth century, escaping the Armenian Genocide in Turkey.

Sima was traveling with her parents, an uncle and two cousins. They were from Ovacik, a small village in the Armenian Highlands. Ovacik was located in a quarter-mile-wide valley on a creek fed by the tall mountains to the north and west. At the time, the village was just beginning to develop as a vacation hotspot for wealthier Armenians living in Tunceli, thirty miles away. Ovacik provided a brief mountain experience in the summer months for those unwilling fully to embrace the reality offered by majestic mountains, including harsh winters. Sima and her family worked in cottage industries making thick, coarse woolen garments for summer travelers.

With the Turkish Government's landgrab and resulting genocide, Sima's family was faced with either moving east, beyond Mt. Ararat to what eventually became the modern country of Armenia, or escaping the highlands all together and seeking refuge in Europe or America. Sima's uncle knew Armenians who had immigrated to the US thirty years earlier and landed eventually in Richmond, Virginia. Sima's family was committed to a new beginning in Richmond.

Yesnich was traveling alone as the only survivor of the Turkish army overtaking his village of Ilic. Ilic was located no more than thirty miles from Ovacik as the crow flies. It was a modest mountain town of no real importance to the Turkish army, except it was on the road though the mountains as the army moved eastward in its efforts to eradicate the Armenians who lived in the region. Though they grew up only thirty miles apart, Sima and Yesnich had never met while living in the homeland. Because their villages were separated by a mountain range, Ovacik tended to look for trading partners south and east while Ilic's interests were north and west in the opposite direction. Roads did connect the two villages; a traveler could travel by road the nearly 100 miles between them by way of Hozat, Cemisgezk, and Kamaliye.

As Yesnich was traveling alone with no particular destination in mind and no connections in the vast country of America, he was open to finding traveling partners. Yesnich happened to bump into Sima's uncle in a long waiting line on Ellis Island. The two started a conversation that led to Sima's uncle inviting the young man to join their group as they made their way to Richmond. Yesnich thought the destination of Richmond sounded as good as any.

After settling in Richmond, Sima and Yesnich began seeing each other on a regular basis. Eventually, they married. Aganetha (Nettie) was born two years later. In the Armenian language, Aganetha means "pure." For Sima, her daughter carried the hope that their new beginning in America could be as pure and fresh as the mountain streams of the Armenian Highlands.

Nettie was a handful from the beginning. She was an incredibly independent child with a flamboyance for the music and dress of the Armenian Highlands, though she had never experienced that culture for herself. With her Bohemian perspective and love of life, she struggled with boundaries.

Sima and Yersnich grew into their new life in Richmond, becoming a central part of the St. James Armenian Church on Patterson Avenue. The church became a cultural center for the growing Armenian community. Remembering their life in Ovacik and Ilic, Sima and Yersnich were strong traditionalists, ever seeking to preserve their heritage even while living in and drawing life from a vastly different country.

Nettie had other ideas. At nineteen, she briefly moved in with her boyfriend, Gus. This terribly upset her parents. Within a matter of a few months, Nettie moved back home and promised to embrace more traditional behaviors. Shortly thereafter, Nettie realized she was pregnant. Gus was nowhere to be found. With few options and overbearing parents, Nettie agreed to leave to "visit an aunt in Harrisonburg," which was code for living with friends of the family and eventually putting her child up for adoption.

Nettie eventually returned to Richmond; in addition to leaving a child in Harrisonburg, she left the happy and flamboyant part of herself there as well. Those who knew her best said Nettie never recovered her happy and free spirit after giving up her daughter.

Nettie's baby was adopted by Henry and Edna Weber, who were active in the Swiss Mennonite Community in Rockingham County, Virginia. They named their daughter Sara, which means "princess." They were delighted to take their new infant daughter to their farm two miles up the valley from Dayton, Virginia; Dayton is a small village on Route 42 between Harrisonburg and Bridgewater. This little grandchild of people from the Armenian Highlands found an unexpected home among the gentle hills of the Shenandoah Valley.

The Weber pair were descendants of immigrants, Swiss Mennonites. Swiss Mennonites generally trace their heritage to the Swiss Reformer Ulrich Zwingle and the Swiss Brethren of Zurich, Switzerland. Swiss Mennonites came from the Anabaptist wing of the Reformation. Zwingle was a strong advocate for stern church worship experiences filled with instruction but lacking completely of music and worship rituals. Swiss Mennonites were characterized by following strict rules, wearing plain clothes, and having a preference for living "separate from the world." They did relax Zwingle's restrictions on music in worship, coming to prefer simple stringed instruments and vocal harmonies.

A wave of Swiss Mennonites responded to William Penn's late eighteenth century invitation to migrate to the newly established Colony of Pennsylvania, and they came there in waves to join the gentle Quaker spirits. Henry and Edna's ancestors were in the first wave of Swiss Mennonites to make the trip and stake a claim for a new beginning in Pennsylvania. With time, the Swiss Mennonite immigrants began to adapt to their new environment, and some adapted too well. It wasn't long before many of the immigrant groups that had responded to Penn's invitation began to experience conflict and division. This was especially true of Russian and Swiss Mennonites. Pennsylvania became a melting pot of ideas about culture and religious tradition.

The mixture of Mennonites who chose to remain in Pennsylvania became the breeding ground for the Amish or merged into other religious traditions established in the colony. Other Mennonite groups that wanted to remain "separate from the world" and uniquely

Mennonite began migrating to other areas of the country. The Swiss Mennonites, with their strict rules and plain clothes, migrated to places like Ohio; Lancaster County, Pennsylvania; and Rockingham Country, Virginia. Henry and Edna's ancestors were among the group that made Rockingham County, Virginia, their new home.

Sara's ancestors, unknown to her at the time, were of a different breed—flamboyant, colorful, loud, and at times glitzy and even ostentatious. To hear Sara tell it, she always knew she was somehow different. Her adopted parents worked hard to discipline the child's spirit. They wanted her to sit up straight and go about life in an orderly way. She wanted to dance. From Sara's perspective, her parents were too strict, unaffectionate, distant, and lacking in flexibility. I suspect her parents thought of their daughter as unruly, stubborn, and unorthodox. Nine-year-old Sara felt a sense of relief when an older cousin teased her about being adopted; this information about being adopted was more long-sought confirmation than news to the granddaughter of the Armenian Highlanders.

One of Sara's earliest memories is of changing clothes on her way to school. Her parents required her to wear plain clothes, but a friend of Sara's was not Mennonite and seemed to have quite a flair for bright colors and flowing skirts. So, on the way to school each day, Sara would meet her friend Mary about a quarter of a mile from Sara's home. Mary always brought several items from her wardrobe—the more colorful the better. Sara would change into Mary's clothes behind a big oak tree and leave her plain clothes there in a bag, and off the pair would go to school. After school on the way home, Sara would change back into her plain clothes. The best part of the story is that Sara's parents never found out about her switching clothes on the way to school.

Sara began experiencing the larger world beyond her strict Mennonite family in sleepovers at her friends' homes. The girls would play the latest records from pop singers of the day. Sara couldn't remember when she heard pop music for the first time at one of the sleepovers, but she did remember the first time she heard the Beatles song, "Here Comes the Sun," on the radio.

At the time Sara did not know the personal circumstances that led George Harrison to write "Here Comes the Sun." Later in their career together, the Beatles struggled with significant conflict in their ranks, especially between John Lennon and Paul McCartney. The conflict became so intense that at one point Harrison left the studio and refused to return for some time. The winter of 1969 in England was particularly cold and brutal. On a more personal level, Harrison was arrested that winter for possession of marijuana and had his tonsils removed. As winter was finally losing its grip, Harrison wrote the music and words to "Here Comes the Sun" as a hopeful indication that a terrible metaphoric winter was giving way to a better and brighter day.

That is what Sara needed to hear.

Beatles songs, and later songs by the Rolling Stones, Led Zeppelin, and Pink Floyd, gave expression to Sara's deep-seated dissonance and afforded affirmation for the spirit in the child and adolescent that wanted to dance like no other.

Once, Sara ran away from home. When she turned sixteen and got her driver's license, she decided to work hard to win her parents' approval. She began a committed effort to live within the confines of her Mennonite family and not lose the privilege of driving the family car, while also maintaining a somewhat different life with her friends, as most of her friends were doing the same. This dual existence went on for several months; even so, her parents never acknowledged her efforts or complimented her for her improved behavior. One morning, she did something to upset her mother; it was so insignificant that Sara never remembered the specific thing that set her mother off. All morning, her mother's scolding went on. The worst part was when Sara drove her mother to a neighbor's home for a quilting party, sitting beside her on the five-minute drive with no way to escape her mother's intense anger.

After dropping her mother off, Sara dove back home and concocted her plan. Her father was out running errands and was to pick up her mother later in the afternoon on his way home, which meant Sara had the family car to herself. She left a note on the kitchen counter explaining that she was running away and indicating that she left the car at the Harrisonburg bus station. In Harrisonburg, Sara went by the bank and withdrew the money in her savings account. At the bus station she purchased a ticket for Richmond, Virginia. Then, at the Richmond bus station, she caught a cab to the Quality Inn, a five-minute drive from a favorite cousin who had left the Mennonite fold three years earlier. She got a room at the motel, went to her room and changed into her swimsuit, and walked down and laid out by the pool to take in the warmth of the sunshine. All had gone according to her plan.

As the sun set and the darkness of night began creeping into her well-laid plan, Sara started second-guessing her strategy. She struggled with uncertainty and finally called her favorite cousin. Her cousin promptly picked Sara up at the motel and took her to her home.

The next morning, Sara's parents arrived, and soon the trio was headed back to their home in Rockingham County. On this occasion, everyone sat quietly. From time to time, sitting in the back seat, Sara would verbalize a gentle sign, to which her mother would respond, "I don't want to hear anything from you. Just sit there and shut up."

Things in the family were different after Sara's escape. Loud arguments became less frequent and were replaced with a simmering sense of reality; everyone was biding time until Sara went off to college.

The day she turned eighteen at the end of May, Sara moved out and moved in with her friend Mary and her parents. Into July, Mary and her parents began getting excited about Mary's college plans. This prompted Sara to consider what she was going to do, as she had previously been accepted at Longwood College but had no money of her own to pay for college. Phone conversations back and forth with her parents created a path forward for Sara: if she moved back home, then her parents would pay her expenses for college. Dutifully, Sara moved back in with her parents for what proved to be two weeks before she left for college in Farmville, Virginia.

Sara lived in Farmville for two years. While her study at Longwood was less than inspiring and she dropped out after two semesters, her time in Farmville provided much-needed direction. After dropping out of Longwood, Sara worked as a clerical employee at a doctors' office for one year. This experience helped her focus on a potential career in speech pathology.

In fall 1977, Sara was in classes at Radford University pursing a new pathway toward a career in speech pathology. Her years at Radford were some of the happiest of her life. She excelled in her studies, kept a busy schedule of extracurricular activities, and generally enjoyed herself.

The year she graduated was the year accreditation requirements changed for a career as a speech pathologist; going forward, she would need a master's degree if she wanted to practice. Without the financial means to move forward with a graduate degree, she took a job in marketing for a group of doctors in Baltimore; she had developed quite a knack for marketing in her work at Radford with the student newspaper.

Sara's Baltimore years were characterized by a growing sense of herself, increased excellence in her professional pursuits, and an improved relationship with her parents. It seems that the distance made for healthier if infrequent contact with her parents. Baltimore also provided the context for meeting her future husband. Bill was a nuclear engineer working at a power plant outside Baltimore, Maryland. Bill was brainy and low-key, which meant that in his presence Sara could play the part of the "star" without competition from him for center stage. He delighted in watching her grab the attention of a small dinner group or work a large room with her extroversion and enthusiasm. He needed some of her excitement and fun-loving exuberance. Of course, there was another side to Bill; by nature and training he tended to focus on parameters, limitations, and details—all of which served him well as a nuclear engineer. Who wants a nuclear power station engineer who doesn't see the blinking warning light on the far side of the control panel?

In their courtship, love, and marriage, there was always attraction and also potential conflict simmering beneath the surface: Sara's need to dance everywhere and all at once and Bill's engineering comfort with clearly establish parameters. Bill loved the clarity of firmly established roles and boundaries. Sarah embraced a flowing, expanding sense of herself.

She and Bill eventually made their home in Charlottesville, Virginia, where their two children were born. Charlottesville also provided Sara with the opportunity to complete a master's degree in speech pathology. In this season of life, Sara was a stay-at-home mom and a part-time graduate student. During this same timeframe, Sara's parents began slow health declines; her mother began showing signs of dementia, and then her father was diagnosed with congestive heart failure. Initially, her mother's condition was manageable by her father, with occasional assistance from Sara. As it was a forty-minute drive from Charlottesville, Sara was able to provide support and occasional help with her mother's decline.

After her mother's death, her father's congestive heart disease seemed to progress more quickly, and her trips back and forth to Dayton became more frequent. Selling the farm and moving her father to a patio home in Charlottesville was both a blessing and a curse. Her father kept changing his mind about selling the property, and when he did agree to sell it, he became obsessed with making sure Sara was not able to access "his money."

Being a mom, working through graduate school, and caring for a grumpy parent took quite a toll on Sara. Then Bill had a heart attack. The heart attack was unexpected though not actually life threatening. However, at the time of the attack it seemed as if Bill was dying. The worst aspect of the heart attack was Bill's personal and emotional reaction to the health crisis. He began to withdraw into himself; the reality of death and one's inability to strategically plan for and schedule its arrival proved very disconcerting to him. The engineer who knew how to regulate and control nuclear reactions was powerless over so much about his health and well-being.

Motherhood, graduate school, a grumpy parent, and a depressed or at least disillusioned spouse proved too much stress on the marriage. While there were some unique features to the breakup, the dissolution of Bill and Sara's marriage followed the all-too-familiar pattern of many couples in America at the time: she needed help with the kids and he was emotionally unavailable; he needed time to work out his inner emotional challenges and she needed someone to get the kids to piano practice; she saw her graduate school graduation as a parachute out of the marriage and he became obsessed with his own internal struggle; she wanted to go to counseling and he refused.

As the kids were leaving the nest, or perched on the edge preparing for college, the mechanics of divorce began to move forward. Eventually, Sara moved in with her dad in the patio home as he became less able to manage his own life. During the year that they shared this home, Sara's delight was her work as a home health speech pathologist. After all the years of preparation and waiting, she was finally doing what she had dreamed of doing: helping older adults regain their ability to communicate. Sara's struggle was caring for a grumpy old man who never seemed to care much for her when she was a child and whose distrust of her made every day a challenge. In many ways his death came as a relief. Finally, it was all over.

The first five years after her father's death were good years for Sara. With her parents gone and her children in college or beginning careers, Sara poured herself into her work. Life was no longer painfully complex. For Sara, speech pathology was always about the patient; she tolerated medical regulations and endless paperwork because they were the price for doing therapy. She found her work as a therapist very rewarding. She loved helping older adults who were deeply appreciative of the life-changing therapy she provided—and she got paid for doing what she loved. Her patients were typically victims of some kind of brain injury or illness, often elderly people recovering from strokes.

One of her patients, Janice, suffered from amyotrophic lateral sclerosis. ALS is often called Lou Gehrig's disease for the famous professional baseball player who died from it. It is a progressive nervous system disease that affects nerves in the brain and spinal cord. It typically begins with muscle twitching and weakness in the limbs, negatively impacting muscles needed to move, speak, eat, and breathe.

Janice was the classic example of the old saying, "You can have all the money in the world, but if you don't have your health…." Janice's doctors ordered speech therapy when she began slurring her words and having trouble swallowing. Sara and Janice were a lot alike—outgoing with lots of friends. When Janice received the devastating diagnosis of ALS, Sara's therapy became more focused on helping Janice prepare for the inevitable, especially since she lived alone. Sara was an advocate for and encourager of Janice. With Sara's help Janice acquired lifting devices to help her with mobility. Next came computer systems so Janice could "speak" by focusing her eyes on a computer keyboard. Through much of her physical decline, Janice was a trooper as Sara cheered her on. When therapy was no longer appropriate, Sara slipped into a friend and volunteer role easily and naturally. Janice died a year later.

After the funeral, Janice's son George asked Sara to come by the homeplace for a few minutes. Standing in Janice's beautiful sunroom overlooking the rolling hills of Virginia's piedmont, George turned to Janice's stellar collection of rare and beautiful orchids and said, "Sara, Mom would want you to have some of her orchids. Later today Mom's children and grandchildren will gather in this room, and each will pick one or more of these plants to take home. Mom would want you to have first pick. Please take two."

Sara has a long history of killing plants. But these two orchids are healthy and vibrant in Sara's modest sunroom. Apparently, the plants have found a happy home.

Most of Sara's patients were in their later chapters of life. Dhrav was an exception. Dhrav and his wife Janya immigrated to the United States from Turkey. Both were natives of Bursa: Dhrav's parents were medical doctors, and Janya's parents were educators. Dhrav was a computer engineering graduate of the Istanbul Technical University. Janya was a graduate of the Marmara University School of Medical Science and trained as a dentist. The brainy couple came to the United States on a student visa. Dhrav had been accepted in Georgetown University's MBA program. After completion of his master's, he accepted a job offer from Citibank in Charlottesville, Virginia.

Dhrav and Janya settled into a home in Hollymead, Virginia, outside of Charlottesville and began making a life for themselves. Within a year the couple became pregnant. They had planned to name their daughter

Ladli (the loved one), but because of the baby's spectacular eyes they named her Vamakshi (beautiful-eyed) instead. Their near storybook life in America came to an end with the birth of a son in October 2017. He was born with a heart defect and required surgery within hours of his birth. The insertion of a feeding tube was an inevitable result of the surgery to save his life. He was given the name Ekavir, "bravest of the brave," because his parents knew he faced significant challenges.

Two months later, Dhrav was in the hospital, having suffered a stroke. Unbeknown to him or his parents, Dhrav had an undiagnosed birth defect, an arteriovenous (AV) malformation in the brain. An AV malformation is an abnormal tangling of blood vessels connecting arteries and veins in the brain. In Dhrav's case, the AV malformation ruptured and caused a stroke.

Dhrav's stroke occurred while he was leading his team in a brainstorming conversation about better ways to create algorithms to identify potential fraud use of an individual's credit card. In the midst of the robust discussion, Dhrav had a sudden headache, slumped down in his chair, and would have fallen to the floor had it not been for the arm of the chair. A team member called 911, and a medical team was onsite within five minutes. During the wait for the medical team to arrive, it was obvious that Dhrav had suffered a stroke: his left side was weakened and he was mentally confused. The medical team quickly transferred Dhrav to the University of Virginia Medical Center.

Janya, home with two children, received a call from Dhrav's supervisor at work alerting her to the emergency. She bundled up the kids and drove to the emergency entrance to the hospital. After nearly an hour wait, an emergency medical doctor provided Janya with a preliminary diagnosis, telling her that Dhrav had suffered a stroke, probably due to an AV malformation. It would be another twenty-four to thirty-six hours before they could ascertain the extent of the brain injury.

After five days in the hospital and two weeks at an inpatient rehabilitation center, Dhrav was discharged home. He continued to have weakness and lack of sensation in his left hand and arm; he could not sense heat or cold. The more critical issue was his impaired cognitive abilities. The stroke disrupted neuropathways in his brain, negatively reducing his reading and problem-solving skills.

Sara was assigned to be Dhrav's home health speech therapist. The first visit was an evaluation was based on the medical diagnosis received from Dhrav's neurologist, but Sara explored concrete and specific limitations of his cognitive capacities. In her evaluation, Sara asked, "Dhrav, if Sally has five apples, then gives one to Mitch and one to Alice, how many does she have left?" Dhrav slightly lifted and looked at his right hand. "Five apples…one apple, two, another apple. What?" He looked at Sara, completely confused. Sara repeated the question. He had no better success the second time around.

On another question, Dhrav could name specific fruits when shown a picture (apple, grapes, orange, etc.) but was unable to offer a reply to the request, "Dhrav, name for me five fruits."

There were also challenges when something required a sequence. "Dhrav," Sara said, "here are four dominos. Place similar numbers together: place the threes together, the sixes, the twos, and so forth."

Dhrav had information in his brain and no significant memory loss, but the pathway to access what he knew was no longer operative. He especially struggled with language. English was not his native language. When asked questions in English, he would think of the answer in his native language and then try to translate into English. This simple, everyday task for someone fluent in both languages became extremely difficult for him.

Sara remembers the stifling sense of fear in the home when she was there for her first visit. Little Ekavir was recuperating from heart surgery, Dhrav from a stroke, and Janya was unemployed because her medical training in Turkey did not allow her to practice as a dentist in the US. Medical doctor training in Turkey does transfer to the US, but dental training does not.

Sara's evaluation indicated that a significant level of improvement could be achieved in Dhrav's cognition if he worked hard. After her evaluation, and sensing just how scared Dhrav and Janya were, she looked at the couple and said, "I know you are scared. I have been doing therapy just like this for years. Dhrav, you are going to get a lot better. You are going to go back to work at some point. We are going to get through this together."

Through years of working with many patients, Sara had realized that hope was a critical ingredient in a patient's success. Regaining cognitive abilities after a stroke can be extremely difficult work. The hope of getting better is the essential driving force that is necessary for significant improvement. If a patient does not believe he can get better, he will not do the work and he will not improve.

Four days later, Dhrav and Sara began therapy sessions three times a week, since creating new neuropathways is a time-sensitive issue. For nine weeks, Sara was in their home three times each week. She was speech therapist and cheerleader. Thereafter, it was twice a week for three more months. In addition to therapy sessions, Sara provided stacks of homework to be completed: cognitive language work, crossword puzzles, and mathematical word problems. Each week the homework became more challenging for Dhrav.

Over the course of months, Sara became the most regular visitor to their home. She bonded with bright-eyed Vamakshi. Janya came to trust her as an advisor on all things medical and as an encouraging helper. Even Ekavir warmed up to her. For Dhrav, Sara was the lifeline to regain his professional life.

For Sara, this was why she became a speech therapist. In the most challenging times, she was able to work with patients and give them a chance at reclaiming their lives.

In the first weeks of therapy Dhrav was still taking two naps a day, as he seemed to be exhausted all the time. Janya attempted to get Dhrav and Ekavir on the same nap schedule with some success.

In time, improvement became more obvious. By late April, Dhrav and his team leader at work were in conversations about his return. Citibank assigned a counselor to Dhrav. The counselor and Sara talked on the phone frequently as the two scheduled a plan for Dhrav to return to work. Initially, he went to work for one half-day each week. Then, it was two half-days a week. In time, he returned to work full-time with his old job responsibilities.

For Sara, therapy was always an investment in a person, not simply a job. Her insistent assurance that "You are going to be OK, and you are going to go back to work" proved to be an inspiration for the struggling pair. After the therapy sessions ceased, Janya continued to check in with Sara. The two became friends.

While there are many stories about Sara's work in speech pathology, the story of the young couple always stuck out in her mind. Single again, with children off in college and beginning careers of their own, Sara's work became her life.

Then came the phone call. The caller identified herself as Mary Jane and said she was Sara's relative: a cousin. It was a strange phone conversation, disjointed and confusing. After a few minutes, Sara was able to understand the purpose of the call. This rambling person on the phone was a relative inviting Sara to learn about her biological parents.

Sara said, "Mary Jane, you know my biological parents were never my real parents. So I have no interest in hearing about them or seeing them."

"Well, they are both dead. I don't guess you want to see them," Mary Jane replied. "But I can tell you where they are buried. They are buried in different places. See, your father—"

"Listen," Sara interrupted, "I am not really interested."

"What about your sister?" came Mary Jane's rejoinder.

Sara froze for a second, then said, "Sister? I have a sister?"

"Well, of course," came the reply. "You see, you are the product of a fling between your mother and father. Lord knows what your mother saw in him. He ended up married to some woman from Kansas, but they were not together long…"

"My sister, you said I have a sister," Sara pressed.

"Yeah, she lives in Orlando. Her name is Susan."

After hearing about a sister, Sara's cascading thoughts became overwhelming. She ended the conversation with Mary Jane, got her phone number, and said she would call her back. The call brought back so many painful memories from her childhood. Sara had always wondered about her birth parents and why they didn't want her.

Now she learned she had a sister. All of this at once was mind-numbing. Sara couldn't wrap her head around it all—she had a sister.

It was a full week before Sara called Mary Jane. She had begun to make the call several times but had not been able to go through with it. She kept thinking that with regard to her biological family, maybe ignorance was bliss. But she finally made the phone call. Mary Jane was much calmer this time around. Sara listened carefully, took several pages of notes, and asked many questions. Mary Jane was the member of the extended family most interested in genealogy; she was interested in names, dates, and family connections rather than in people and their stories. Consequently, Sara collected the bare facts. She did indeed have a half-sister, Susan, who lived in Orlando and worked as a business writer for the local newspaper. Sara's mother, Aganetha "Nettie" Hagopian, had married Michael Arakelian in 1959 (two years after Sara's birth). Susan was born the following year in late 1960. Michael died in 1991, and Nettie died in 1995. Sara's mother was Armenian. Mary Jane had talked to Susan on the phone two years earlier. At that time, Susan knew she had a half-sister; she found the paperwork from when the child was put up for adoption in her mother's documents after her death. Neither Mary Jane nor Susan had a way to contact Sara, as they didn't know her name or where she lived. Mary Jane had only located Sara the day before her first call, thus all the excitement on the phone. And maybe most importantly, Mary Jane had Susan's phone number. After Sara hung up the phone following the second conversation, she sat in silence. She realized that the doors to her past and future had both opened at the same time.

It was a full two weeks before Sara called Susan. She chose mid-afternoon on a Sunday. She dialed the number and a perky voice answered, "Hi, you have reached Susan. I am not available. Leave a message and I will call you back." Then, of course, came the annoying "beep."

Sara started talking. "Hi, I am…my name is Sara. This is really awkward, but I received a call from a Mary Jane who said that I might be your sister. I am not sure if this is true or not. It all is new to me. If you get a chance…"

Susan immediately pickup up the phone, interrupting Sara's message. "Hello, this is Susan." There was a pause and Susan continued. "So you talked to Mary Jane? I am sorry; I didn't get your name."

"My name is Sara."

"My name is Susan. Well, I guess you know that. Where do you live?" Susan asked.

"Ah, I live in Charlottesville, Virginia."

Susan said, "Yes, this feels really strange. But were you born in Harrisonburg on May 31, 1957?"

"How did you know that? Yes."

"I found your birthplace and date of birth on documents in my mother's things after her death. You really are my half-sister," Susan said with surprise and wonder.

The conversation between two long-lost sisters became a contest of who could ask the most questions in one phone conversation. They exchanged information, phone numbers, addresses, hair and eye colors, height, not-so-much weight, and a variety of other seemingly trivial information.

Susan suggested that they should meet in person. "Think you might be able to come to Orlando?"

"I would love to," Sara replied.

Over the next few days, a date was identified that would work for both sisters. Sara looked forward to her weekend trip to Orlando.

The flight to Orlando went off without a hitch. Sara arrived on time and began making her way through the complex and busy Orlando airport, shuttle ride and all. The plan was to meet in the baggage claim area. Of course Sara had checked a bag; she always overpacked—extra outfits and shoes for unexpected opportunities.

Susan and her husband Jeff stood on the baggage claim level of the airport at the bottom of the escalators descending from the airport arrival gates. They both watched as people two stories up stepped on the escalators and came down to pick up their baggage. Susan held a sign reading, "Welcome, Sara!" so the two sisters could find each other in the crowd. Susan continued to scan travelers on the escalators.

She instinctively lowered the sign as her eyes fixed on a woman halfway down. Jeff reached over to grab the sign and lift it.

Without changing her gaze, Susan said, "Oh my god, she is the spitting image of my mother." Jeff was bewildered. Susan walked to the escalator, leaving him holding the sign. As Sara stepped off the escalator, Susan threw out her arms for a long-awaited hug.

It was an excellent weekend.

Sara made four trips to Orlando specifically to spend extended weekends with her sister. Susan made three trips to Charlottesville. The two hit it off wonderfully. Sara could not have been more pleased: finally, a family member who was not crazy and was an absolute joy to spend time with. It was a deeply healing relationship for Sara, as if something ancient in her was now at peace.

Sara remembered sitting and talking with Susan. Sometimes the conversation would turn to the mother Sara never knew. Susan favored her father more than her mother in looks and disposition. As a child, Susan had also tended to identify more with her father. She remembered her mother as a "flawed and unhappy person most of her adult life." The marriage to Susan's father may have had some romance and passion early on, but if so, it had lost much of its luster by the time Susan was an adolescent. Susan did note that finding out she had a sister helped her better understand her mother. For instance, Susan remembered her mother saying a few times, "I always wish I had had another daughter." Susan also remembered her mother getting upset when a neighbor's child went missing for a few hours. "Mother was in a state of panic, while the rest of us knew little Charlie would show up. He always did."

One day the pair walked around Lake Eola in downtown Orlando. It was a beautiful day, one of those bright and sunny Florida days. Sara remembered the many swans that populated the lake and its surrounding park. Sometimes they would simply stand on the concrete walkway and force people to move around them. Sara learned the hard way not to try petting the birds. The swans, of course, were looking for food, a French fry or piece of bread from the street vendors or those who bought a snack from them.

Sara enjoyed her time with Susan, just soaking up being in the presence of someone who shared much of her DNA and had an everyday connection with her mother.

On one of Susan's visits to Charlottesville, Sara delighted in planning their weekend together. Shopping and a pedicure were a must; Sara offered a number of other options for their few days together. She always thought it was a bit unusual that Susan had no interest in visiting their mother's grave site. This stuck in Sara's mind because she had been to her mother's grave on several occasions, wishing she could have known her. Susan, on the other hand, had lived with their mother and now had no interest in visiting the grave.

Sara could not help noticing Susan's gazes. In moments when the conversation died down or when they were busy watching a favorite TV program, Sara would catch Susan staring at her. Susan seemed fascinated with Sara, her looks, the way she tilted her head, her physical mannerisms, the way she used her hands—all of this seemed uncannily familiar to her.

At times, Susan and Sara mused about taking a trip together. Once, in a small shop they saw a brochure advertising a "Lazy Trip Down the Mississippi." The trip was on a Mississippi steamboat with the big paddle wheel in the back. There were a number of beginning and destination points for three-day, four-day, or weeklong trips. The sisters thought this adventure might well be in their future.

Through her fifty-six years, Sara had experienced some measure of joy and happiness but more than her share of loss, disappointment, frustration, and judgment. Yet the news of Susan's sudden heart attack and death sent a massive quaking trimmer to the core of her being. After finding joy in her sister—and a large measure of peace with her past—this death brought forward the vilest fears from Sara's personal story. Her sister's death was devastating news in itself; how horrible for a vibrant, fifty-two-year-old woman to die suddenly from a heart attack that no one saw coming. For Sara, the loss was magnified by a deep, existential sense of abandonment that every orphaned child knows: "those who should love and protect me are going to abandon me; it is only a matter of time."

Shock is an adaptation of the human species; it provides a foggy, slow-motion mental state in the face of overwhelming circumstances. In effect, it helps us manage horrific circumstances without a total meltdown or shutdown; we humans are not equipped with circuit breakers that can simply shut off when overwhelmed with demand.

Sara experienced shock, as did all of Susan's family and friends. Making funeral plans, attending the funeral, and walking through the next few weeks as Susan's affairs were resolved, those closest to Susan began to see pathways forward. Yet the mental fog of shock remained for some months for Sara as she wrestled with the deeper issues of her particular life story. Most of the time, we just motor along in life, adapting to joys and sorrows similar to how planets alter their trajectory based on the gravitational pull of massive stars or gigantic planets. Susan's death was a bit of a black hole for Sara, threatening to gobble up life itself.

Like her mother Nettie, Sara found a way forward even in the face of insurmountable odds. Plodding along at a less than joyful pace, Sara continued to find solace in her work. In her personal life, though, things were not going well. Her divorce from Bill had significant ripple effects in her relationship with her children. While Bill had been unwilling to go to counseling to work through marital problems, he felt abandoned as Sara sought the divorce. Bill didn't want to move forward. He continued to blame Sara for the divorce and ascribed little responsibility to himself for the failure of their marriage. On holidays, Bill refused to be in the same room with Sara, which put their children in an awkward position. After the divorce, Bill played the part of the "wounded dove," emotionally limping around around the children.

The children reacted differently. Their son distanced himself from both parents and became self-absorbed in his own professional life in Seattle, Washington. He rarely came back to the East Coast and rarely connected with either parent. Their daughter Mary sided with Bill. Interestingly, Bill had never been very involved in his children's lives. In many ways he had been an emotionally absent father. After the divorce, however, Mary and her father Bill became closer.

Sara's failed marriage and troubling relationships with her children created significant distress. For Sara it was the return of an old, old story: abandoned and now alone. It was a lonely way to live.

A girlfriend encouraged Sara to consider dating, saying that maybe there was someone new for her out there. Sara thought she might give it a try. She dated a few men but found the "pickings to be slim." Many men her age were not interested in meaningful relationships, and Sara was not looking for a casual fling.

Truth be told, finding a new someone in the late sixth or seventh decade of life tends to be rare. For people in these later life chapters, finding someone becomes exceedingly complex. Young adults find one another, fall in love, and grow up together. Older adults have children, sometimes grandchildren, houses, and bank accounts. The two most important predictors of marital success for people who find love in the later chapters of life are financial compatibility and their children's approval; "loving each other" comes in at a distant third! Of course, with adult children there are different levels of support for a parent's remarriage. Some are absolutely against a parent remarrying later in life; in some cases, it has something to do with potential inheritance. Other adult children claim to be supportive of mom or dad remarrying but always seem to find fault with particular prospects. For conscious and many unconscious reasons, adult children have trouble being truly enthusiastic about their parents finding love later in life.

Given the complexities of building a new love relationship in one's later decades, many people settle: settle to remain alone or settle to be with someone who makes sense for every special interest party involved.

Sara wondered if she would find a new love in her life or if she would just "settle."

Walt

Now we come to my part in the story. My great-great-grandmother's sister, who dipped snuff (tobacco), was known as the only woman in Gates Country, North Carolina, who could sit on the couch and spit into the fireplace. My older sister discovered this bit of information while looking for royalty in our ancestral family tree.

I descended from a colorful and complicated lot. Of course, I did not know that in my growing-up years. At the time, my family of six lived in a two-bedroom home of 795 square feet on a gravel road in Portsmouth, Virginia. Since everyone else in the community was as poor as we were, we all assumed we were living the good life.

The "good life" of living in Portsmouth, Virginia, in the late 1950s had roots in two different directions. My mother's family were the Whites of Alexander County, North Carolina. John White and his wife Elizabeth originally settled on Walnut Knob, fifteen miles north of Taylorsville overlooking the Little River valley in early 1805. Moving south to begin a family with a man she barely knew but deeply loved was challenging for Elizabeth; the big walnut trees reminded her of Grandma Day's old homeplace in Virginia.

The Walnut Knob property was purchased from the estate of William Granville, grandson of Lord Granville, one of the heirs of the eight Lord Proprietors who in 1663 was issued a charter for all North Carolina, South Carolina, and Georgia by King Charles II of England.

Seven of the Proprietors sold their shares of what was called the Carolina Province back to the king. Lord Carteret, later the Earl of Granville, insisted on having his one-eighth of the province. Lord Carteret never visited his lands in the New World, though he enjoyed having conversations at elaborate parties about his extensive land holdings in the Carolina Province.

In due time, the land holdings in Carolina Province passed on to William Granville, heir to the dwindling estate of Lord Carteret. William sought a fresh beginning for his family in the New World, traveling to Charleston, South Carolina, and then up to his holdings in North Carolina.

Though William Granville owed a considerable amount of land, he was not wealthy. He began selling off as much land as possible to acquire capital for a modest plantation in the eastern part of North Carolina. The mountainous terrain of what would become Alexander County held no interest for William Granville. Unfortunately, he was unable to find buyers.

At the time of William's death in 1804, the land in Alexander County remained unsold. In the months after his death, his heirs moved to sell massive portions of land in the estate as quickly as possible.

John White acted uninterested in Walnut Knob and ended up getting the land for a bargain. In fact, a bargain was all he could afford. The White home, built on a small outcropping on the western edge of Walnut Knob, was a one-room log cabin with a lean-to attached to the side for children to sleep in and for storage. This is as far back as I have been able to trace my family heritage on my mother's side. Family tradition suggests that John White relocated to Alexander County from the western part of Pennsylvania, but there is no documentation to that effect. What is known is that the White side of the family were simple mountain people with an appreciation for moonshine.

The Crafford side, my father's family, originally lived in Gates County, North Carolina, on marshland near the Chowan River. The Craffords were river people. Even though my grandfather left the banks of the Chowan River in his early twenties for greener pastures, fifty years later his favorite breakfast dish remained "fish heads and rice"; he left the marshlands, but, apparently, the marshlands did not completely leave him. Our family heritage has been traced back to an Abraham Crafford in the 1790 census data for Gates County. Pushing back beyond that date is nearly impossible, as the Gates County Court House burned to the ground and with it historic records prior to 1790. Some family stories suggest that Crafford was an assumed name, the original surname being Crawford. Other stories connect my heritage to a Peter Crafford in the Jamestown settlement of 1607.

Some trace their family heritage to aristocrats, business tycoons, royalty, or hardworking farmers. My heritage on both sides of the family seems to be among the "don't ask, don't tell" crowd. As my son the civil engineer says, "It is what it is."

My family's life changed significantly in 1963, when my father decided to become a minister. Prior to his call to ministry, my father worked as a "shade-tree mechanic" at a gas station and volunteered as a fireman at the local fire station. Later he went to night school to become a second-class radio and TV technician. His call to ministry posed several challenges for my family, not the least of which was how he would get and pay for the training needed to be a minister.

At eleven years of age, I was not privileged to know the inner process involved in making the necessary decisions. Soon enough, I learned we were leaving Portsmouth and moving in with my grandparents on a farm outside Orange, Virginia, and my father would commute to a Bible College in Western North Carolina, 400 miles away.

This change of geography brought my grandparents, Clarence and Molly, into my personal story; in time, both became critical and essential people in my personal, emotional, and spiritual development. For all practical purposes, my grandparents became additional parental figures for me.

To put it in distilled form, my mother was not affectionate or emotionally available; my father, after his call to ministry, was strict, self-focused, and wanted his children to comply with his dreamed future; by contrast, my grandmother gushed warmth and affection while maintaining an air of accountability and order; and my grandfather was an honest, hardworking, and gentle soul. At times, I wished my grandparents had been my parents.

Of course, in my preteen years I had no clue about my emotional and psychological development. Instead, I was busy discovering farm life. My younger brother and I tried to domesticate wild kittens, and we have the scars to prove it. We rode small pigs and learned to run fast to escape the big ones. We threw rocks at chickens and learned to avoid the roosters. We tried to catch small fish with our hands while standing knee-deep in the stream down the hill from the house—no luck on that effort. We also learned about the seasons and rhythms of nature. We cared for animals of all sorts and learned the responsibility that goes with stewardship. For two city boys moved to the country, the farm was rich in new and exciting adventures.

After his graduation from Bible College, my father began his ministry career preaching at a church some fifteen miles from where we lived. Over the years my father pastored a number of churches. In his early ministry he rarely stayed at one church more than three years; it seems he either served some really divided churches or his style brought out the worst in the congregations. I remember my dad noting in his later life that every time he moved to a new church, he accepted a reduction in salary; for him, this truth was a "badge of honor" attesting to his faithfulness. For the first twenty years of his ministry career, he remained in "entry-level ministerial work"; this had a significant impact on family finances.

Even so, I have many fun-filled memories of my growing-up years. The positive memories center on childhood friends and games, large family gatherings, Sunday lunch at Grandma's home, and a host of affirming and positive experiences with my four siblings. Several memories are critical in terms of how they impacted the way I think about myself.

After my father "got religion" and attended Bible College, our family had daily devotions. We would gather as a family to eat breakfast, although no one was allowed to start eating until every family member was seated at the table. After a blessing by my father, we ate our meal. After clearing the table, we sat down again at our places for our family devotion. We took turns reading the assigned text for the day. Thereafter, my father would share some insight that came to his mind from the text. He would invite others of us to offer any insights that might have come to our minds, which we rarely did. Then he would either close the devotion in prayer or call on one of us to pray. All in all, the family devotion took from five to eight minutes.

I am sure the idea of a family devotion came out of my father's experience at Bible College, a practical implementation of the "family that prays together stays together" philosophy. With all due respect, I am sure this devotion time reflected my father's attempt at being the spiritual leader of the family and providing religious instruction for those under his care. In large part, I think us kids just tolerated this new emphasis in the family. Personally, I took a wait-and-see attitude toward my father's spiritual leader focus. My dad wasn't nearly as much fun to be around after he "got religion."

Prior to "getting religion," my father *was* fun to be around. I remember going with him on Sunday afternoons to a local school playground. The school has since been demolished and the property was sold to a developer; today it is the site of the Victory Crossing Shopping Center. On our outings together, we would fly remote-controlled airplanes. At the time, my father enjoyed building and flying these planes; this hobby was an outgrowth of his training as a TV technician. We would spend three hours together every week. I was his helper.

I also helped around the TV repair shop, cleaning floors, straightening up, and taking out to the dumpster old TV parts that were no longer useful. From time to time, I would go with him on home visits to repair TVs. Many a time I stood in front of a TV in someone's home holding a mirror so my father, crouched behind the back of the set, could make adjustments. Occasionally, my dad's adjustments were sufficient. Most often, they were not. In the 1950s, TVs were composed of two primary pieces: the outer wooden cabinet and the inner metal chassis to which all components of the TV's electrical system were attached—the picture tube, speakers, and electrical circuits. In the majority of cases, my dad would remove the inner metal chassis and take it to the repair shop. The metal chassis contained the essential TV and all its working parts and, of course, was much smaller and easier to transport than bulky pieces of furniture.

Prior to his religious renewal, my father didn't attend church; he used to be found on the couch asleep when my mom and us kids returned from Sunday school. After his spiritual awakening, his religious commitment to family devotions and other family matters seemed contrived and artificial—at least that was my impression. It seemed he was "doing the right thing" out of an intellectual conviction because someone he admired had told him he should do it, as opposed to the "right thing" growing out of his personal mission, values, emotion, or affection. Sometimes my dad reminded me of an actor reading lines and portraying a character in a play.

A significant event in my teen years cast an unnecessary shadow over much of my life as a young adult. I share it only because it illustrates the kind of family I grew up in and the natural consequences of that kind of environment.

I must have been fifteen years old because I remember it as the year before I was able to get my driver's license. I went to a Friday night football game with a friend from church, Jill, who lived a mile from our home. She was just a friend, and I caught ride with her to the game. As was customary in those days, after the game there was always a sock hop, a dance. I thought we were simply going to the game and returning home. Once there, I think Jill wanted to check out a guy, and so we stayed at the dance for maybe forty-five minutes. This was significant because it was the first dance I attended as a teenager and because attendance at dances was strictly forbidden in my family by my "spiritual leader father." It seems that in Bible College, my father developed a clear list of things that were unacceptable for Christians—things that would put you on a slippery slope to destruction. Dancing was one of those things; in this perspective, dancing was an early stage of foreplay. In the uneducated, fervent religious subculture I grew up in, this made reasonable if not perfect sense. For me at the time, the dance was a terribly awkward event: I stood around for a while, talked with a few guy friends, and danced once with a girl, largely because a friend told me she had a crush on me.

Because we stayed for a while at the dance, I arrived home about an hour later than my father expected. He was waiting up for me.

"Where have you been?" he asked.

I replied, "I went to the game."

"Don't get smart with me," he retorted. "Where did you go after the game?"

"I didn't realize it when I got a ride with Jill, but Jill wanted to stay for part of the dance after the game. So I didn't really have a choice about what to do."

"Did you go into the dance?" he pressed.

"Yeah, I did." I didn't say the rest of I was thinking: "What was I supposed to do, stand outside in the cold?"

Quickly and lethally, my father said, "If you ever go to another dance, when you get home your bags will be packed and on the porch for you." With that, he was off to bed in a huff. I wasn't shocked or devastated by his words. Rather, his words in that moment seemed to confirm what I had been experiencing with the "spiritual leader" character who had replaced my dad. It confirmed the random and ill-informed thought in my head that I was welcome in the family as long as I complied.

The dancing confrontation became the seed of a twenty-year grudge I held against my father. When it happened, I embraced my new perspective as instructive for how I needed to manage my rather tenuous place in the family: I needed to conform until I was old enough to make it on my own. The truth is, my father never really meant what he said that night; it was just words a worried father says when he doesn't know what else to say. Filled with worry for my well-being because I was late from the game, he inappropriately expressed his frustration with no real appreciation for how it might impact me.

More importantly for me at the time, based on the previous several years of our family's life, I thought he was completely serious. I thought that, in an unguarded moment, he had revealed his true self, his new self.

Regardless, the dancing confrontation became the seed, the splinter, of my twenty-year grudge. I never intended for the memory of the confrontation to become an infection in my spirit, but it did. I thought often of the confrontation and played it back over and over in my head. From that day forward, I thought I had gained a real insight into the reality that was my life, as opposed to the play that was being acted out by my father.

Through the years, as I learned more about psychology and appropriate parental behavior, I resented the way my father had reacted to me during the dancing confrontation. I brooded over the events of that night.

Infection of any sort brings natural consequences. If it is a wooden splinter, we feel discomfort; a bit of pus will develop at the site of the invasion. The injury is annoying and troublesome until the cause of the infection is dealt with and extracted. Only then can healing begin.

I let the infection go on for twenty years. I didn't act out against my father as much as I bided my time and simply lived in the emotional confines of my family. Even so, the infection took its natural toll on me. I developed a psychological distrust of authority figures. I would get annoyed with police officers who pulled me over for speeding—not a particularly helpful strategy in that situation. I became skeptical of people when I met them for the first time; I always looked for a deeper, truer self behind actors in the drama of everyday life. Trusting others was a chore for me.

The summer after my junior year of high school, I coached a little league baseball team. I was paired up with a middle-aged man named Jess. Jess wanted to be involved with the league as he thought it was a good program for developing youth in the rural county where we lived. As it turned out, Jess was a man of some financial means. We had a successful summer of baseball and won the championship. As an end-of-the-year party, the team was invited over to Jess's home. Jess owned a small airplane and had his own grass airstrip. He took players up for a short ride. Of course, I too enjoyed the brief ride. It was the first time I rode in an airplane.

Once back on the ground, Jess called players and coaches over in a group for one last huddle. He handed out gifts to all the players.

Then he said to all of us, "I have one last present to give, but to get it you have to give me twenty dollars."

We all wondered what this unusual gift might be. And of course none of the children had twenty dollars in their pockets. "Something special for twenty dollars. Who wants this special gift?" Jess repeated several times.

No one spoke up. Finally, Jess turned to me and said, "Do you have twenty dollars on you?"

I nodded, but I wasn't about to turn lose my hold on a twenty-dollar bill. Then, Jess began unrolling his unique gift in front of us. It was two one-hundred-dollar bills—the first time I saw a bill that large.

This story has stuck with me for fifty years, maybe as a memory reflecting my distrust of others. Jess and I worked together as a pair that summer. He wanted to be supportive of little league in the area. He had learned that to be successful, he needed a younger accomplice, someone who could inspire the kids and create excitement on the team. I was that guy in the summer of 1969. And I missed my first two one-hundred-dollar bills because I was unwilling to trust a man I had worked with for several months.

Interestingly, my learned distrust tended to be focused on men, not women. For instance, in a group of guys I tended to think all the macho talk was about simply following a socially acceptable script; all the chest-beating and huffing and puffing was just an act. In a group of women, or a mixed group (when guys are not in their element), I felt more trusting; I sensed that people were being their real selves, maybe their better selves.

I wondered why people couldn't just be their better selves all the time. After all, isn't the better self the real self? This was the idealism of my young adult years. In time, I would learn that the better self is more what people aspire to as opposed to the real self, which is closer to being self-focused or self-centered.

In my mid-thirties, I had a chat with my father about the dancing confrontation. At the time, I was a reasonably accomplished pastor and had spent too many years in graduate school attempting to satisfy an overactive curiosity. I described for him the events of the night of the dance. He asked me to tell the story again, which I did with a little more enthusiasm.

I shall never forget his response: "Walt, I have no memory of the events you are describing."

While I did not anticipate this response, I was not surprised. I guess I confronted my father in the hopes he would own his comments and apologize for his words and behavior. I suspect this is what everyone wants who has ever been wronged in some way, big or small. But it is the response victims rarely, if ever, get. People who say or do cruel things are the very people who will later have no memory of the injustice; it is just the way insensitive people are wired.

The confrontation with my father was helpful for me. I had lived through a perceived trauma and come out stronger on the other side.

I escaped my family by going to college. Initially, I wanted to be an engineer and enjoyed the problem solving and science associated with engineering. In my third semester, I switched out of engineering to prepare for a career in ministry. This decision grew out of a prolonged struggle over what I wanted to do with my life. While engineering was appealing, I longed to be in a guardianship role, caring for the church as a farmer cared for the ecosystem entrusted to him, including his family. Many years later, I would come to grips with the way my career choice brought together isolated and segmented aspects of my personal story; in seeing my life's calling as being a "guardian of the church," I was combining the roles of my father and grandfather. Ministry was a way to heal my soul. As I said many times to seminary students preparing for a career in ministry, "You are here focused on saving people, and the first person you are trying to save is yourself."

After college and before graduate school, I married my high school sweetheart, Maggie. We shared different and yet similar experiences in early childhood, including poverty and dysfunctional families, hers more so than mine. Over the years of our marriage, we were in and out of marriage counseling a number of times. Our happiest years were our earliest years together, before the arrival of our children. The births of our sons and the resulting parental responsibilities brought up issues from our own childhoods that were challenging for us as a couple. It is an old and well-rehearsed saga: starry-eyed lovers decide to have children while avoiding all the mistakes their parents made. In the process of birthing and parenting, they avoid the mistakes of their parents and make a whole new set of mistakes they never envisioned. It is called being human.

Other significant challenges presented themselves with the births of our granddaughters. I jokingly said about Maggie, "She has some DNA stuff going on with those granddaughters." In truth, there were deep issues at work: the birth of granddaughters brought forward unresolved physical and emotional abuse Maggie had suffered in her childhood years. It was interesting that these specific issues didn't arise with the births of our sons. In Maggie's family, boys were to be tough and had to learn to take care of themselves. On the other hand, girls were vulnerable and needed to be protected and defended.

Grandma became protective, defensive, and quick to identify potential injustices to her perfect granddaughters. Her new vigilant protection of her granddaughters created unacknowledged tension between her and her sons and daughters-in-law. It also upended the "old married couple" routines we had settled into. Of course, I saw myself, inescapably, as the guardian of my family, and so I plodded along doing what was required to keep us as happy as possible. These struggles were at the heart of my decision to retire at age sixty-five and a half; I had always wanted to work until I was seventy. I retired earlier than planned as a way of coping with the increasingly challenging circumstances of my private life. I am not unusual in this regard; rarely does the seventh decade of life go as we envision. We energetically declare that seventy is the new fifty, all the while knowing that older life is on a mental and physical decline—sometimes gently, sometimes rapidly. In the seventh decade of life, we all make our peace with our new reality, one way or another.

My sense of guardianship extended to my public life in ministry. It seems I had a knack for helping congregations and institutions in trying circumstances. This became obvious in the last half of my ministry career. In my early forties, I became senior pastor of a large church that had just gone through the troubling exit of its former pastor. The pastor had several inappropriate relationships with female members of the church, and the way the church's lay leaders forced the minister out created deep and long-term anxiety in the church. I remember several friends saying to me as I contemplated becoming the church's pastor, "Walt, don't do it. That situation is nothing but trouble."

But I saw myself as a gifted guardian who could create healthy ecosystems, so I interpreted the advice of my friends as reasons I *should* take the job. The church needed my guardianship. I took the position knowing the well-established trend in congregational life: after a misbehaving pastor and congregational trauma, the next pastor gets blamed for the church's problems and tends to get fired within five years. There are always exceptions to this general rule; sometimes people step into such situations and things work out really well. In either case, I took the job thinking to myself, "I am going to help this good church through a hard time." Within the first year of taking the job, I realized things were not going to "work out really well," at least not for my career. On the outside, the church maintained a sense that everything was going well. On the inside, there were a lot of hurt and unresolved feelings in the members of the church related to the former minister and to the way his departure unfolded.

While things were going reasonably well in the church and its many ministries, there was a lack of ease in the relationships I shared with elected congregational leaders. Of course, getting used to the new pastor is an adventure for every church. In the Nashville church, the complexity was multiplied several times over by the church's recent history. Into my second year at the church, a few odd incidents quietly convinced me that I would not stay at the church for the next twenty-five years.

During my years there, I often publicly referred to the church as an "uncommonly good church." It was in every regard, even though it had been through a rough few years before my arrival. Based on my personal journey and perspective as a guardian of the church, I began planning for a six-to-eight-year sojourn at the church. I wanted to get the church to a better place and then gently step aside and let another person move into the pastoral role; I began making the way smoother for my successor. While it was theoretically possible, I did not entertain the other option of staying for twenty-five years. The longer stay would have required me to upend much of the church's structure and life. This very thing had happened in the Nashville church thirty years before my arrival. A pastor took a hard, uncompromising, strident stand on the racial divide of the 1960s. The pastor's position (welcome integration) and, more importantly, strident stand took quite a toll on the church. Many families left the church in the early 1960s primarily because of how hard the pastor pushed on the issue; a gentler approach could have caused much less trauma. That particular pastor stayed twenty years. In the first few years, the church lost several hundred members, which it slowly began replacing in the ensuing eighteen years. All told, the pastor who stayed twenty years saw the church's membership numbers increase by a handful of families over those years.

I saw no reason to put the Nashville church on such a roller coaster. The better option for the church was for me to get the congregation to a better place and then simply ease out of town to a new opportunity for myself.

I stayed a total of six and a half years. I did develop many healthy relationships in the congregation and found the years in the church to be good for my children. All in all, I enjoyed "pushing the bolder up the hill" to get the church to a better place. There is something to be said for hard work, whether it is physical or mental. The greatest satisfaction for me was to watch my successor's success at the church, as I lived several states away at the time.

Later, I became pastor of a church in Orlando, Florida, that was trying to reinvent itself in line with emerging twenty-first century trends. This proved to be a lot of fun as we explored innovative and creative approaches to ministry. I became pastor of this congregation in a season when the church was hopeful, relatively happy, and full of enthusiasm. To no one's surprise, these years of service were among my happiest and most rewarding.

In large part, my years of active pastoral ministry were immensely rewarding. While much of pastoral ministry is routine and perfunctory, it also allows for deeply personal and intimate emotional connections with people and their struggles. This is the part of pastoral work that I thrived on, dealing at a deeper level with people. When your two-year-old child is diagnosed with cancer, all that is frivolous and superficial in life evaporates as people, not actors, wrestle with the deepest mysteries of life.

As a pastor, I developed a real knack for doing funerals. I used to say, "I would rather do three funerals than one wedding."

Nothing is more superficial than most modern weddings; on the other hand, funerals deal with the most profound realities of life.

Like all pastors, I have a long list of great stories to tell about church members, myself, and the role of ministry.

I remember my first funeral. It was graveside only, for a church member's brother who was homeless, gay, and died alone at night on a street in Los Angeles. The temperature at graveside in North Carolina was twenty degrees and the wind was blowing—and as a poor struggling seminary student, I did not own an overcoat.

At a different church, I was preaching one Sunday on the need of our congregation to cultivate a supportive and loving sense of community and a memory flashed into my mind as I was speaking; I could almost see my grandmother in her beloved vegetable garden cultivating with her well-worn garden hoe. So on the spot I sought to weave the sermon's idea into the image of my grandmother in her garden. I skillfully introduced the garden image into the general theme of the day and was so focused on the image that I forgot sometimes words have dual meanings. In front of God and my congregation I said, "We need to work the garden of our church. We need to till the soil with our garden hoes. I am telling you, we would be a better church if we had more hoes around here. We need more working hoes in our church." Apparently, it was a very memorable sermon for my church members.

Not related directly to my ministry, but a part of the tradition that seemed to follow me in ministry, there is the carousel swing ride story. Most of us are familiar with the carousel swing ride at the local amusement park: chairs are suspended by chains from an overhead carousel. As the carousel begins to turn faster and faster, centrifugal force pushes the chairs and occupants into ever larger, higher, and more angled circles. Keep the image in mind.

The home we lived in when our boys graduated from high school featured a steep backyard. The backyard area closest to the house was flat, as a bull dozer had carved out a level place to build the home. About forty feet beyond the house, the backyard was a steep incline of clay. I got the bright idea that we should terrace the backyard and make beautiful flower beds in place of the steep, ugly clay incline.

I had a bundle of large landscaping timbers delivered. Even large timbers on a clay incline have to be solidly anchored. So, with shovel and pickax, I started trying to hand dig vertical holes for anchoring posts. In the clay and rock, this was nearly impossible.

My next idea was to rent a gas-powered post-hole digging auger. The hydraulic kind that you tow behind a car wasn't a possibility, as there was no way to get it up the clay embankment. I opted for the most powerful two-man auger, with a six-horsepower engine. Two guys at the rental center loaded it in the back of my SUV. Once home, I found that the engine itself was too heavy for me to get out of the car, let alone carry up the hill. I enlisted my football-playing-son to help me carry it and the auger up the hill. That was two trips.

We assembled the monster, set it upright, and got it centered in the modest six-inch-deep hole I had started earlier. Our first approach/test was simply to start the engine, hold firmly to the handles on opposite sides of the engine, and see if the engine's weight was enough to cause the auger to penetrate the clay and begin digging out the hole. No luck. The auger turned and ended up smoothing out the clay like a flat saucer. Our second approach was to put body weight on the handles, forcing the auger into the clay. This only made a smoother clay surface in the hole.

On the third try, we put nearly all our combined weight, at least 300 pounds, on the handles and went wide open on the engine throttle, which brings me back to the carousel swinging chairs. The football player let go pretty quickly. The too-long-in-graduate-school father did not and began spinning round and round with the auger and landed on the ground with a loud "thud."

I never told this story to anyone, but it seemed to follow me wherever I lived.

Pastoral ministry is some of the most meaningful work one can ever do. You embrace people at the highest and lowest moments of life. You become part of a person's emotional family and support system. There truly is something sacred about the work of ministry.

There is also, of course, the underbelly of the church—the part of the church that is less obvious and often hidden from sight. People are people, and so church members can be small-minded and cruel in the most sanctimonious ways. I found people in my congregations who were actors, people playing parts that I knew represented an idealized view of themselves they wished to present to the world. There were church members who were profoundly needy, and the local congregation became the stage on which they sought to act out their need. The church is no different from any organization in that some use the church for their own twisted and distorted purpose. Even so, among my church members over the years I found some of the most honest, authentic, and spiritual people I have ever met.

The last ten years of my ministry career were devoted to a small financially struggling seminary; again, I was seeking to hold the school and its community together against declining trends in the number of people who wanted a seminary education. The shift to the administrative and strategic work of an educational institution was a bit of a transition, but I thrived on the interaction with people. Given to generalizations, I can say that in becoming a seminary president, I traded deacons for faculty members and came out on the short end of the stick. While I have the deepest respect for the role faculty play in the teaching/learning enterprise, I found that faculty presented their own unique challenges. Before becoming a seminary president, I talked with three experienced seminary presidents. I asked each of them, "What is the most challenging part of leading a seminary?" All three responded with the same answer: "Faculty tenure." I agree. Having actors in the mix who for all practical purposes could not be fired or would not rotate off a committee created a monkey wrench in my effort to create a healthy ecosystem in the school. While my years at the school were rewarding in general, I trudged through some aspects of my work and delighted in others, especially in the students we sent off as graduates.

In the summer of 2015, Maggie and I started looking at cities and towns we might move to in retirement. Orlando was an obvious possibility, as we had friends there and the grandkids would always want to come see us along with Mickey and Minnie Mouse. We visited Charleston, Savannah, and Columbia—all in South Carolina. I was interested in expanding the search, but Maggie was set on being within driving distance of our children. In addition, in retirement she was interested in expanding the time she spent on a golf course.

More than once I said of her, "The woman is addicted to golf." I blame Susan Dale, an Orlando friend, for getting her interested in golf. After Maggie started playing golf at fifty years of age, she seemed to live for the sport. She regularly volunteered at golf courses so she could play golf for free. Beginning with our thirtieth wedding anniversary, every wedding anniversary trip was a golf trip: the Kohler Courses (Wisconsin), Whistling Straits (Wisconsin), Bandon Dunes (Oregon), Teeth of the Dog and Punta Espada (Dominion Republic), Arcadia Hills (Michigan), Chambers Bay (Washington), Pinehurst (North Carolina), Pebble Beach and Half Moon Bay (California), several British courses, and on and on the list went.

I remember saying to her with some frustration, "Once, I would like to go on an anniversary trip to a US city and not play golf." To which she replied in earnest, "What would we do?" I didn't say it but I thought, "What every other tourist does when they visit that city."

It was well known to friends that we were contemplating retirement. It was equally well known that after family moves rotating around my career choices for all those years, Maggie was going to make the ultimate decision about where we lived in retirement. She obviously enjoyed her decision-making power.

I announced my retirement from the school in February 2016. Five weeks later, Maggie died in a car accident. At the time of the accident, she was doing some part-time consulting work in North Carolina. On her way back home on US 360, at the intersection of Virginia Route 624, her car veered off the road and hit an oak tree. The coroner's report indicated that she died almost instantaneously from head trauma related to the crash.

Over the years of ministry, I had read many books about grief and walked with a hundred and more families through the "valley of the shadow" of loss. In the end, grief sucks. It is horrible, terrible, and life-crippling. The only stage of grief is constant. Grief is like an ocean wave; it swells, washes over us, and then gently subsides, and the waves just keep coming. Over time they become less threatening, and we learn better how to keep our balance in the relentless cascade of memories.

My grief was complex, as it is for most people and families. Wrapped up with the loss of my spouse, and all the trauma that event inflicted on my extended family, was the assault on my personal sense of identity—the guardianship thing wasn't working in its most important realm, my family.

In addition, I was troubled by the circumstances of Maggie's death. What caused the accident? After her funeral, I went back to the intersection where she died several times, trying to piece together how the accident happened. There were no black marks indicating that she had locked the brakes. Did she doze off? Did she black out? Did she veer to miss a car pulling out from the intersection? There were no text messages or phone calls on her phone prior to or during the accident. It was upsetting not to know what caused the accident. Mystery at the death of a loved one only complicates grief.

For the benefit of readers who did not know Maggie or never visited the scene of the accident, I am confident that it was not intentional on Maggie's part. In all our ups and downs, there was never any indication that Maggie would hurt herself. And the accident scene argued against it as well. Maggie's car went through the intersection into a ditch and hit a steep bank on the other side of the ditch. Anyone looking at the scene would think that a person who ran off the road there would just hit the dirt embankment hard and either stop or "climb" the bank and come to a stop among the small trees that dominate the site. Maggie was driving her large SUV. Apparently, her SUV hit the dirt embankment and bounced upward because of the SUV's heavy-duty suspension hitting the oak tree some four feet off the ground. No one could have predicted that outcome.

And then there was the other issue complicating my grief: I never got to say goodbye.

As a retired minister, I know the difference between widowers who handle grief well and those who do not. I was determined to push through grief on the "well" side of things. After Maggie's funeral, I developed an intentional routine to help me get through my grief.

I would not recommend this to others, but it worked for me. As an early riser, I devoted an hour to an hour and a half every morning to processing my grief. I journaled, I replayed critical events of my loss (learning of her death, remembering the funeral, and having phone conversations to tell family members about her death), I walked around the house and talked out loud about how I was feeling. These sessions included weeping, anger, and laughter—sometimes all within five minutes. I followed this routine without exception. In addition, I sought the advice and help of a counselor.

As I think back over that season of my life, the word "resignation" comes to mind. I never wanted to be the guy who suddenly lost his wife. I never wanted to have my world upended. I never wanted to imagine moving into the twilight of my life solo. I was also thankful that I wasn't the guy who died six weeks after his wife's death, overwhelmed with grief.

All in all, I was resigned to my new life going forward. Life had been good for me. I had accomplished a good bit in my sixty-five years. I assumed I would remain unmarried, maybe find a female friend to go out to dinner or to a movie with me. If I did remarry, I assumed it would be years down the road and focus primarily on companionship; as Bonnie Raitt sings in "Luck of the Draw," I would be thankful "we get along."

After my wife's death, while still working at the seminary, I began laying out my retirement plans. Most ministers retire and then go back to doing the same thing they have always done; they preach for pastors on vacation and take part-time jobs in pastoral care or pastoral visitation. Whether working or as a volunteer, most pastors center their lives in a church somewhere.

I thought of retirement as a new chapter opening in my life, not simply the continuation of the previous chapter. Some of this was certainly because of the death of my wife and all the dynamics that were altered because of her death. The larger part of it for me grew out of my lifelong tension between actors and their underlying real selves. I knew well how those realities played out in the life of the church. I wondered how they played out in other arenas of life. I hoped that the next chapter of my life would include more honesty and less acting, for myself and others.

I decided to move to Charlotte, North Carolina, in retirement. I had a son who lived there and the city was between Raleigh, North Carolina, and Birmingham, Alabama. With family members in those two cities, Charlotte felt like a good location to begin more honest living.

As one who prides himself as being a planner par excellence, I began sketching out the transition to the Charlotte area. In early October, my son and I bought season tickets to the Charlotte Hornets' games (NBA). As I knew I would be traveling to Charlotte from time to time in planning the transition, I thought it might be fun to catch a few basketball games; my son and I agreed to sell the seats when we were not interested in attending particular games or if I was not in Charlotte when the games were scheduled. Buying season tickets was not one of my better investment decisions.

In addition, I began searching for apartments. As there are normally waiting lists to get into Charlotte's more comfortable apartments, I knew it was necessary to select where I wanted to live and get on a waiting list. As I planned to retire June 30, I was looking at a rather short timeframe for relocation.

While in Charlotte looking at apartments, I also began pursing possible long-term options. I wanted to live in an apartment for a year to get more familiar with the area before making a purchase of a home or condo. At that point, a condo seemed a good option. I was particularly interested in condos in Fort Mill, South Carolina. Fort Mill is just south of Charlotte. Living in that area was a way to be close to Charlotte and avoid state income taxes; South Carolina has no state income tax. My backup plan was to relocate in Rock Hill, South Carolina, a few miles south of Fort Mill.

Yes, I am a planner. I like to lay out my options and give careful attention to significant decisions. While I didn't have all the details, I was fully committed to a concrete plan: move to Charlotte, North Carolina, and begin my retirement chapter. It is great to have a plan!

Sara and Walt

I taught graduate courses online. I thought, surely, I can figure out how to do an online dating profile.

As part of my planned strategy to make Charlotte my new home, I began thinking about what my life as a single man might look like in the future. I anticipated remaining single for some time as I was rapidly approaching my sixty-sixth birthday and fully planned to take it slow on all matters related to the opposite sex. Having known many widowers over the years in my pastoral work, I knew it would be challenging to meet someone given my perspective on life: fiscally conservative and socially liberal, educated but holding dear the simple things of life, similar backgrounds but not too much so, and financially compatible.

While these complexities were at the forefront of my thoughts as I planned my move to Charlotte, in the back of my mind was a more gnawing concern: was I emotionally ready to meet someone new? It is amazing what you can find on the internet. Sharon is a relationship specialist living in the Charlotte area with an expertise in assessing whether a person is ready to find a new someone after the death of a spouse. I couldn't believe there were people out there with such specialized training.

I contacted Sharon through the internet and we agreed on an assessment package; yes, you pay for this service. I took an extensive assessment questionnaire online and then went to Charlotte to spend a few hours getting a report on the questionnaire and being interviewed by Sharon. This was a helpful way of confirming my progress in processing my loss. It also began to help me think more realistically about my future. In addition, from Sharon I got one of those eye-opening quotes that, for me, was distilled truth: "Always tell the deep truth about yourself. This is not about confessing dark secrets; it is about being authentic, being yourself at the deepest level possible. In the things you say and do, live and speak in harmony with your deepest self. If you do this, you will attract similar souls. Truth be told, you don't want a relationship with someone who is fundamentally at odds with your essential self."

Given my adolescent challenges with actors playing parts, I found Sharon's words life-centering. With this mantra in mind, I researched online dating sites. I discarded many that focus on casual dating and hooking up with strangers. I settled on one that focused on educated people looking for longer-term relationships, either serious or not so serious. As I was unsure of how serious a relationship I wanted, I thought this site would be a good match for me.

On a Sunday afternoon, I decided it was time to work on my first ever online dating profile. The work I did with the relationship coach was helpful as I began filling in the dating profile. Her words, "always tell the deep truth about yourself," informed my writing as I worked on the form. With time, I selected appropriate pictures and was well past sections about things I liked and disliked. I was also careful to note the things that were "extremely important" to me. I wanted a narrow search.

I was probably two-thirds of the way through the profile when I decided to take a break. Before leaving the profile, having learned the hard way the importance of saving your work, I noticed a small button in the upper right-hand corner of the screen: "Save." So I hit the save button and went off to take a break from the profile and finish a few chores around the house. One thing led to another, and it was a few hours before I returned to the computer. What I didn't know at the time was that the "Save" button was also the publish button. When I hit "Save," my profile went public on the site.

At literally the same time I was filling in the profile, in another town a woman named Sara logged on to the dating site to search for a way to unsubscribe. She had been on it for a couple of months and met a few guys, all of whom seemed nice, but it just wasn't working for her. As with all online enterprises, it is harder to unsubscribe than to subscribe. As she searched through the unsubscribe maze, the computer screen noted that she had a new match. She read through the match and found it somewhat interesting. On a whim, she casually responded with a "like" on my profile comment about small-mindedness.

The particular question was, "What do you dislike in others?" I answered with, "small-minded people"; Sara's answer to the same question was "narrow-minded people." She noted that we shared a similar view on people we tended to dislike.

This was actually a big deal for Sara. In the typical online dating process, taking the initiative in beginning a conversation with another person is significant. This is particularly so for women: does a woman begin the conversation or wait for the man to initiate it? It is the old dilemma of who asks whom out on a date. Well, Sara had always played the more traditional role of waiting for the man to begin a conversation. On this occasion, however, she was looking to unsubscribe, so she figured why not comment.

I pulled up my profile page, assuming I would reengage and finish it. When the screen appeared, I was not looking at the profile entry page but at a new screen I had never seen before. It took a moment for my brain to realize I had been matched with a real-life person. I was horrified. I thought to myself, "OMG, what have I done!" The experience was so disconcerting that I put aside the computer and walked outside for some fresh air.

Returning to the site later, I began working feverishly to finish the profile. I was especially pleased to see the question about location at the end of the profile. With some satisfaction, I listed my geographic search area as limited to Charlotte and 25 miles around Charlotte, and I categorized this as "extremely important."

I felt a sense of calm come over me as I finished the profile. Now I had posted the profile that better articulated my interests, including the all-important location of Charlotte. After saving/publishing, the screen returned to my matches.

I looked at the handful of pictures and thought again to myself, "What have I done!" All of the matches were in the Richmond area, which held no interest for me. Having read and reread procedural matters on the dating site, I knew my options: I could acknowledge the "like," acknowledge and ask a question, acknowledge and offer a similar "like" for something my match had in her profile, or ignore her "like" altogether. I pondered what to do. My pastoral training had taught me to always respond to phone messages and texts, so no response was not a likely response for me.

Finally, I responded with a simple, short comment. I was polite but not "chatty."

As a guy in my sixties looking only for a meaningful and possibly long-term relationship, I attracted more online attention than I had expected. On that first day, I was matched with ten or more women in the Richmond area, most of whom had liked something in my profile. I quickly realized that, as I was not interested in staying in the Richmond area, I had best not respond to their "like"—regardless of what it might suggest about me. I had responded to my first match in Central Virginia, Sara, and I was resolved not to make that mistake again. Having replied to Sara's "like," I decided to respond only when I received a comment or question from her.

In the coming weeks I was matched with women in the Charlotte area. I read through profiles several times and always responded to those who had liked some part of my profile. I did not initiate any conversations with women online, primarily because I was committed to taking the process slowly. For six weeks I continued several conversations with women in the Charlotte area. I planned to visit my son and his family in Charlotte around Thanksgiving and thought I would stay a few extra days and maybe meet one or more of the women I was communicating with through the dating site.

While I was intently focused on the Charlotte area, I still had a conversation going on with Sara. I decided it would make sense to meet her for coffee or dinner. I assumed meeting her would resolve any lingering thoughts I had about pursuing a relationship with her.

We met for dinner, and I was amazed at how easy our in-person conversation went. She and I share the same quirky sense of humor and found that we clearly had much more in common than I imagined from our online conversation. I remember leaving the restaurant thinking, "If the people I meet in Charlotte have this much in common with me, this online dating thing might work out."

After returning to Richmond following my extended Thanksgiving weekend in Charlotte and meeting several women in person, I reflected on where I was in the dating process. I had certainly met several women in the Charlotte area who were impressive in many regards, and I thought I could possibly have a future with several of them. Even so, I did not meet anyone in Charlotte like Sara; from the beginning we had an emotional connection and a comfortable sense of peace and calm in each other's presence.

I decided to turn my immediate attention to Sara and explore more fully with her what an ongoing conversation/relationship might look like. While I thought a deeper relationship with Sara might be a possibility, I thought it was a slim possibility.

Of course, men tend to be three steps behind women in matters of romance, and that was certainly the case with Sara. She had sized me up much more quickly than I could possibly imagine. She patiently waited for me to embrace the obvious new dawn. For months I had been on a complicated journey to see if I could find the right person to share the twilight chapter of my life; I searched the dating site, I traveled to adjacent states, I had too many "identity verification" coffee dates, I calculated and double-checked for personality traits of matches produced by an algorithm that did not know me. And all the while Sara waited patiently for me to do whatever searching I needed to do. In the moment I chose her, I realized she had chosen me months before.

We planned a weekend getaway to Wintergreen; it was our first time spending a weekend together, and we were both a little anxious about it. One of the highlights of the weekend was tubing down a snow-covered slope. It was a lot more fun than it sounds. Sara had a hip replaced nine months earlier and I have a long history with knee injury, so skiing was out of the question; alas, there is wisdom in knowing your limits as you get a little older.

Prior to leaving, we dropped Nita off at the vet. This fifteen-year-old, eleven-pound dog had been a constant companion to Sara through divorce, death, and the beginning of a new relationship. Mostly, Nita slept a lot when I was over at Sara's home sharing a meal, painting a deck, rearranging attic storage, or replacing a faucet. Upon initially meeting Nita, she gave me a brief sniff and then pretty much ignored me. Occasionally, she would lift her head as I entered the home, but mostly she was disinterested. One cold winter evening, while I stood drinking hot caffeine-free tea in the kitchen, she meandered through my legs and feet on her way to her water bowl. She drank from the bowl in the licking motion as dogs do, and then she just walked out a different kitchen door and back to her bed in Sara's bedroom—all the while acting as if I didn't exist.

I have never been a lover of dogs. They seem like a lot of trouble to me, especially when you take a trip and have to make arrangements for their boarding. Through the years I noted how people would leave lunch or a church meeting early because they needed to get home to let the dog out. It all seemed too restrictive to me. Sara, on the other hand, loved dogs. On walks through the nearby park, we would meet someone walking a dog. Sara would always ask permission to approach the dog. She would pet, stoke, and talk to the dog as if the dog were a human being. To see Sara love a dog made me wonder if I was missing something, like in the Matrix movie series where the world around you isn't the real world. While I occasionally wondered, I remained noncommittal about dogs and pets in general. The truth is I never felt any connection to a dog; there was never anything emotional in having a dog around. It didn't soothe anything for me the way it did for Sara.

We dropped Nita off at the vet because she was having some health problems. She was staying in her bed most of the time, not eating well, and seemed to have discomfort with walking. The vet had suggested that a few days at the kennel could help him evaluate her. She was, after all, fifteen years old and toward the end of her life.

The day before we left Wintergreen, the vet texted Sara to note that Nita's health was declining. Sara and the vet texted back and forth for a few minutes. I could tell the news was not good. The next morning, we bundled up our things and headed home by way of the vet to check on Nita. When we arrived, it was obvious that the staff had been waiting for us. We were ushered into a small consultation room, and soon the vet appeared without Nita. He immediately noted that she was in the back resting comfortably.

Then he said, "Sara, you have been bringing Nita here for more than a decade, and you know that I am a great optimist about the health of dogs. I remember several years ago when you brought her in with that infection in her leg. You wondered if she could survive and I assured you we could make her well and we did. Well, today I have different news. Nita is not going to make it through this time. I am seeing signs that her organs are beginning to shut down, and I don't recommend that we try to extend her life."

Sara took the news well. I sat there in stunned silence. I remembered all the times I visited church members in nursing homes, and they were hanging on to life by a thin thread. Sometimes when I was preparing to leave, the patient would say, "Now pastor, before you go please say a prayer. And pastor, I want you to pray asking God to take me on home to heaven." I had often stood by hospital beds with patients who were kept alive by breathing machines and gave no indications that they were aware of their surroundings. Out of experiences like those, I had become a quiet advocate for non-resuscitating orders and end-of-life directives. Too many times, I had wished the medical doctors would have said to family members what the vet said to Sara. There comes a time when it is time.

Apparently, Nita's time had come. The vet left and returned in a few minutes with Nita. I watched as Sara took her "baby" in her arms. I was beside Sara with my left arm gently around her shoulder. I watched as Sara talked to Nita, cooed, and gently nudged her with her nose. She stroked her head and began reciting all the adventures they had shared over fifteen years. Watching Sara, I remember thinking to myself, now that is the way everyone wants to be loved.

It wasn't long before Nita stopped breathing; it was a gentle moment, a moment of relief. The vet began talking about how they would take care of the body. Sara said a burial was not needed. She had shifted into her medical professional mode of making sure everything would be taken care of relative to Nita's arrangements. The vet mentioned that we could take care of necessary measures at the reception desk as we left. That was my cue.

I left the room and went to the reception desk and offered my credit card. The bill was $1,167.45. I had always heard of pet owners paying thousands of dollars on a pet's care, but I never thought I would be one of them. In a few minutes, as I completed the necessary measures, the door opened from the consultation room and Sara walked out alone. I took her by the hand and we went out to the car. Sara was a distracted trooper; she seemed to be at peace and sad at the same time.

The next morning, I was up early and reading the news on my iPad when Sara came into the kitchen. I asked how she was doing, and she indicated that she was okay and relieved that Nita had not suffered longer. Then, again in that medical mode I love, she started listing a few things she needed to get done during the day. She said, "I need to go by the vet and take care of Nita's bill."

"I took care of that yesterday," I said.

"How much was it?" she asked.

"I don't remember," I said.

She smiled and said, "Thank you."

"Gladly," I responded.

She wasn't surprised that I had paid the bill; that's when I knew Sara was a "keeper."

A year and a half later we were married in a small, family-and-friends-only wedding—in Charlotte of all places. We chose the location because it worked well for family members as a central location. Charlotte also offered a nonstop flight to Aruba, where we went for our honeymoon.

In Aruba, we stayed at the Manchebo Resort. It is in the low-rise section of Aruba—low-rise because the buildings are two to three stories as opposed to the larger, taller resorts to the north. Manchebo offered daily yoga classes that Sara thoroughly enjoyed, but she never went to the sunrise class! It was a wonderful week away.

The highlight of the trip was Sara's idea. "Let's rent a jeep and drive around the island," she said. Well, we did, and it proved to be a delightful day. We literally drove all the way around the island, snorkeling at a handful of sites along our journey. The trip also allowed us to see what most people never see in Aruba, the eastern coast. The west coast of Aruba has wonderful sandy beaches and gentle waves. The east coast is basically lava rock that makes the sand-covered ground hard, so there are no paved or gravel roads on that side of the island. In the jeep we drove on well-worn paths down the coast. The waves hit the rocky edge of the island hard, resulting in tall splashes of salty water.

As we approached the southern part of the island, paved roads reappeared. We did not have a map of the area given the poor phone reception, so we just kept turning onto ever larger roads headed south. The final snorkeling site at the southern tip of the island proved to be our best experience of the day.

On the flight home, I remember reflecting on all that had transpired in my life in three years: sudden death of a spouse, retirement, finding a special new person in my life, and now marriage. The only part of that I had anticipated was retirement. As I watched Sara, she turned and saw my gaze. "You are the best thing that ever happened to me," she said.

I can hardly believe all that transpired during such a short time. Mostly, I am amazed that I found Sara, and my twilight chapter will be one of the happiest of my life. Life is good—sometimes excellent.

Brunch Conclusion

Being a guy, it took me a few moments to realize there were two rings on Mia's finger. Sara saw the wedding band right off and said with exuberance, "So when did you get married?" I was still in the mental fog of two rings. "I thought the wedding was in December," Sara added.

Mia replied quickly, "We got married yesterday with a justice of the peace in Fancy Gap."

The mental fog got a bit denser for me. I was sorting through the implications of this new revelation as Mia and Sara chatted and bantered back and forth like middle school girls filled with excitement and joy. Carlos just sat across from me with a big, manly grin on his face.

A good bit of my mental fog was because a wedding conducted by a justice of the peace, without an entourage of family and friends, seemed contrary to everything I knew about Mia and her Puerto Rician heritage.

When my first wife and I had moved into our home in Orlando, Mia, who was a member of the church I was to serve, came over to our home and helped us unpack. She spent hours in our kitchen having the best time unpacking every box labeled "kitchen" and organizing the contents into drawers and cabinets. She took over the task with great excitement, and all the while she carried on multiple conversations with me, my wife, and the movers coming and going as the truck was unloaded.

I also remembered the day Mia's daughter was married. I had officiated the ceremony, which was fairly brief and streamlined yet still a fully appropriate and delightful event. After the bride and groom processed to the back of the assembled gathering of seventy-five people, a celebrative party broke out. While I had designated the follow-up event as a "reception," traditional Anglo Southerner that I am, it seems that everyone else in the assembly recognized it as a party. The only thing that comes close to it is the rambunctious part of the movie *My Big Fat Greek Wedding*. It was quite a celebration in the best traditions of

Puerto Rico, an eye-opening experience for me. The exuberance, the demonstrative expressions of deep emotions, and the energetic partying exhausted me as I sat in a corner and watched all the happenings.

I had anticipated that Mia and Carlos's December 12 wedding would also include wonderful celebrations, in spite of COVID-19 restrictions.

But now, sitting in the booth at the Crooked Oak Café, it all made sense. If a pandemic doesn't allow a big party at the wedding, then do something out of the box like getting married with a justice of the peace in Fancy Gap, Virginia!

I finally caught up to the booth conversation about their wedding and plans for the future. It was refreshing to embrace their marriage and the long and at times lonely journey that had led Mia and Carlos to this new, better place in life.

Apparently, Sara and I were the first to learn of the marriage of Mia and Carlos. And they had planned it that way. Before they made the announcement to family and friends, they wanted me to "bless their wedding."

"You are partly responsible for us marrying," Mia said to me.

I was speechless. I didn't know what to say.

"Do you remember the time I came to your office and talked with you about moving forward with plans to divorce my husband?" Mia asked.

"Yes," I replied. "But I don't just now recall the details of the conversation." The office conversation Mia was talking about must have happened eighteen to twenty years before our conversation at the Crooked Oak Café. Truth be told, my memory of that original conversation was meager; I could barely recall that she came by my office one day.

Well, no need to worry; Mia could remember it all, and at points she quoted exactly what I had said in the conversation so long ago, lost in my memory.

The larger context for our office conversation was related to Mia's long struggle with her first marriage. Her husband's issues with depression and PTSD were becoming unbearable. Mia, dutiful wife that she was, stayed in the marriage far longer than anyone could possibly expect. She went the sixth, seventh, and eighth mile with her first husband. Her pain had become so obvious to her friends that everyone who knew Mia at the time wished she would just walk away from the marriage and start over. It was as if Mia was the last to admit what everyone else knew: that her first marriage was irretrievably broken and was sucking the life out of her.

The immediate context for the office conversation was a sermon I had preached the Sunday before. Apparently, I had preached about the importance of staying true to one's commitments. Though I have no memory of the specific sermon, I imagine it was a message about commitment to family or the mission of God in the world or some similar theme.

"Do you remember what you said to me?" Mia asked.

I gave the bewildered look honed by most ministers to suggest we don't have a clue.

Mia continued, "You said to me, 'Mia, over these long years of struggle you have shown your children what it means to stay. Now you need to teach them enough is enough. You need to show them what it means to begin anew.'"

While I did not remember saying this to Mia, I recognized it as something I would likely say. I also recognized it as consistent with what I had learned over the years of being a pastor. Sometimes ministers say things to receptive parishioners well beyond what they intended to say; that is, sometimes a person's words become a Word from God for a parishioner. Apparently, that was the case for Mia.

We talked for the better part of an additional hour at the Crooked Oak Café, long after our meal was complete and the waitress had taken our plates. We began to wind down the conversation in preparation for our four-hour journey home and Mia and Carlos's continued "honeymoon."

Mia and Sara began chatting and brainstorming about a special way for me to bless the marriage. The four of us headed out of the café and searched for an appropriate place for such a blessing. Just past the gravel parking lot was a grassy, level section before the ground dropped off significantly. Carlos began setting up a tripod and attaching his iPhone to record our little event. Sara busied herself, checking to make sure the bride looked her best. Then, all of a sudden, Sara ran back into the restaurant. She returned with a long string of white paper towels she had acquired from the bathroom. She quickly folded and refolded the paper towels to make a large bow with trailing ends. This she affixed to Mia's hair. Carlos and I found a place for the blessing that overlooked the beautiful mountains in the distance; we had to position the camera carefully to avoid getting the overhead power lines in the video.

We stood there at the edge of the parking lot with mountains in the background just as I had stood at the church's altar so many times with other couples. Mia and Carlos faced each other, and I stood near, looking at both of them. Sara pushed the start button.

In an abbreviated wedding ceremony, I reminded Carlos and Mia of the journey they had traveled to their moment of marriage. Each of them had faced hardship and disappointment, but now they shared a magical moment and a bright future. I noted, "We are not here today by casual accident but by divine appointment. God has brought us to this sacred place today. Not only do Sara and I bless this marriage, but more importantly God blesses this marriage, as God has been at work in all our lives for healing, redemption, and hope." With that, I offered a simple prayer of blessing, asking God to guide Carlos and Mia in all the days to come.

Then, we all hugged and laughed. As I hugged Mia, I noticed over her shoulder that a small group of locals had gathered outside the café's entrance to watch us from across the parking lot. I immediately thought of a few lines of Elizabeth Barrett Browning's poem:

> Earth's crammed with heaven,
> And every common bush afire with God:
> But only he who sees takes off his shoes.
> The rest sit round and pluck blackberries.

Well, the four of us were not plucking blackberries that day. We were dancing on the sacred ground of God's provision.

Thirty minutes later, Sara and I were headed down US 58 East toward our home. No words were needed. We both were filled with joy. We were thankful that Carlos and Mia had found one another after such difficult journeys in life. And we knew, somehow we knew, that God had been drawing them together as a way of bringing healing into the deepest places of their hearts. And, of course, in celebrating the happy circumstances in their lives, we also came to sense that their story was our story. Out of loss and great disappointment we had found a new lease on life and love in our sixties—when neither of us thought it was possible.

Sara turned to me and said, "I would not have missed this for anything. What a beautiful day!"

www.ingramcontent.com/pod-product-compliance
Lightning Source LLC
Chambersburg PA
CBHW071007160426
43193CB00012B/1959